Marketing Mindset

How to Build a Strong Business from the Bottom Up

Peter Matisko

Author: Peter Matisko, PhD

Book cover and graphics: Anastasia Krol

Translation from Czech: Lena Macrie Hunt

Editor: Cole Pruden

Edition year: 2020

First English edition

ISBN: 978-80-908014-0-0

Contact: book@marketing-mindset.net

Web: www.marketing-mindset.net

www.cyberma.net

III

Contents

Why Was This Book Written?

We Have A Goal – Success. What Is It?

Many books and guides promise different paths to success, and by success, they usually mean money. By closely relating success and money, we unwittingly create psychological barriers to satisfaction. People can do great work at a job they enjoy, but still feel that they don't live up to the societal ideal of a successful person. This influence can cause people to leave a job they enjoy to achieve success on another path that is less fulfilling or even makes them unhappy.

To understand success, we must first define it. Here are a few points that I believe characterize a successful person, as well as some cliché factors that really don't matter.

Success is a state of mind, set of values, and lifestyle of doing work that is enjoyable and fulfilling – work that keeps you up late at night and gets you out of bed again in the morning. An individual (or company) is successful when it benefits other people, creates value that makes life easier for others, and can inspire and empower personal development.

Money should never be the main target of any endeavor. Money won't make you happy while at work, won't overcome your personal obstacles, or motivate you to move forward. Even with money, you can feel empty and burnt out. That's why it's important to build a career that is personally fulfilling. It's not necessary to look for a high salary or prestigious position. It's meaningless to collect material items that serve no purpose other than to advertise our status. It may bring a sense of importance at first, but soon it will become clear that others don't care what car you drive or if you carry a Gucci handbag.

I know some great people who make a lot of money, but you would never guess it. They rent their apartments, don't have cars, don't wear expensive jewelry. Instead, they use their income to travel, get to know people, and have new experiences. At thirty, they have already traveled the world.

These are the people who want to build something, whether in science, technology, or society. Their goal is to improve the current state of knowledge and bring innovation. Money is not the main goal. If they have money, they are willing to invest it. Of course, ideas and business plans sometimes fail, but that doesn't deter them. These people keep going forward, overcoming obstacles, and developing. The internal growth and opportunity to face new challenges provide the feeling that what they are doing makes sense.

We should keep in mind that there's nothing less engaging than spending 10 hours a day doing work we consider unnecessary, and neither a company car nor a dizzying salary will fix that situation.

Everyone's success is individual, but it's always accompanied by hard work. There is no way to make a valuable output that serves someone else by looking for loopholes or the path of least resistance. Hard work brings results when we enjoy doing it. The secret is finding what activity fulfills us.

Marketing is a tool to help us achieve success. While we must see the meaning in our work, we also must see the greater economic picture. Creating products that don't serve anyone or are directly negative won't enrich us in any sense of the word. We must think economically in both business and employment.

Why Do We Need Marketing?

We all imagine something when we hear the word *marketing*: television ads, online advertising campaigns, social networking, flyers, billboards. In our everyday lives, *marketing* is the parade of flashing advertisement banners, videos we have to skip to get to the article we want to read or content we want to watch.

Companies like using terms such as *marketing strategy, surveys, advertisement,* or *sales tactics.* Internet projects are equipped with all sorts of tools, such as visitor analysis, client behavior on the page, visualization of sales funnels, heat maps… The list goes on and on.

Why do we need all of this? Simply because we want to sell our products and services to someone and generate a profit. Who stands in our way? Primarily our competition, whether direct or indirect. However, we also have to consider the role that psychology plays, it has a strong influence on decision-making and a consumer's willingness to spend money on a product or service. Resistance to spending is strong and can't be overcome by rational arguments alone. People often behave irrationally, but the good news is that this irrationality can be used in our favor, as it is usually well predictable.

Because *Marketing* is a very popular concept, many people feel that they understand it intuitively and that there is no reason to spend time examining the theory more closely. When they start businesses, they do not seek out foundations and principles, but instead, search for miracle tools that are supposed to do all the work. This, however, never pans out the way they hope, inevitably ending in business failure.

Marketing is an extraordinarily dynamic field, which is constantly changing and developing alongside societal values, the emergence of new technologies, and access to new products. You may not be aware of just how much shopping and overall purchasing behavior has changed over time. Mainstream access to internet shopping has yet to reach its twentieth birthday, still, it's managed to completely transform our purchasing habits. Despite new influences, people retain their "human nature" and haven't transformed into robotic purchasing machines. Purchasing decisions are still influenced by emotions, relationships, recommendations, and the crowd effect. In many ways, consumers still behave irrationally and make many illogical decisions.

If you find yourself getting caught up in all the available marketing tools and are still searching for the "right" one, stop for a moment. Let's go back to the basics together. You'll see that everything you learn will help you make more effective decisions and achieve better results.

Numerous marketing books and short e-books are devoted to different tools and tactics. The authors of these publications describe what worked for them and how a particular method helped them achieve great sales and business success. It could be anything – a guaranteed strategy for Twitter or Facebook, some unique tips for advertising with Google Ads, a complete guide for email marketing, among many other possibilities. Readers of these books hope that if they carefully repeat the marketing procedure described, they too will have great success, or at least results similar to the author's. Unfortunately, this scenario doesn't play out for most people, and no strategy works exactly as described in a book. There are many reasons for this, but the primary issue is these books are simply incapable of describing absolutely everything. A book rarely discusses favorable preconditions or gets into the complicated web of decisions and circumstances that contributed to the individual author's successful outcome. It's like building a house, then publishing a book on how to build walls and roofs, while failing to mention that the construction itself relies on a quality architectural design for the project. And not only that – behind the project are many people with practical experience, talent, and imagination. In short, many things may not be visible, but still fundamentally essential.

The Strength of Marketing is In Mindset And Attitude

This book, *Marketing Mindset*, focuses on the essential foundations of successfully running a business and marketing to clients. It's about **attitude**, your method of working, and **marketing mindset**. We want to introduce a system of reasoning, which will help you create a successful business on a solid foundation. Once you have this, all other books about marketing tools will become way more useful because you will understand *why* and *how* the methods they describe can be applied.

We'll use many examples to illustrate how marketing works in practice. In this book, we'll not only go over presentation, but also an attitude, and the proper approach to customers, ourselves, and work. Together, we will get acquainted with important factors that influence our decisions and those of our clients – emphasizing the importance of communication with the target market and a detailed understanding of potential clients and the way they make decisions. Moreover, this book will connect the concept of marketing to whatever endeavor fulfills and brings you joy.

This book is not intended to merely introduce you to a strategy you can take, repeat, and achieve success. As you'll soon find out, no such universal strategy can even exist because each entrepreneur and project are different, and the starting positions vary considerably. We won't be describing some blueprint you can use to achieve rapid growth. Instead, the goal is to help you build a strong foundation, which may not be visible at first glance but is nonetheless essential. As always, the bigger you build, the stronger and more sophisticated your foundation must be. This ensures the work will continue to stand the test of time and not fall to the ground at the first sign of pressure or shock.

Why even bother dealing with such basic notions as concepts, attitudes, and theory? Isn't it a waste of time? Isn't it too abstract? The most famous business authors, such as Napoleon Hill, Simon Sinek, Stephen Covey, Robert Kiyosaki, and others, built on the idea of having the proper motivation and outlook on life. They would say that success begins in the mind, and the primary manifestation of a successful person is in his or her approach. This doesn't mean putting blind faith in success, but rather in determination, and doing things that make sense.

There are many interesting parallels between successful people across varied disciplines. These people are distinguished not only by determination and persistence but also by a *sense* for business opportunities. How do they do it? By being interested in potential clients and gathering information they can later put to good use. Apple, for example, completely changed the industry of selling music by paying attention to the desires of consumers. They changed the market by selling what the customers wanted. The opposite can be true as well. Nokia had previously controlled almost 50% of the world market but fell to the bottom in only a few years[1]. Despite large budgets and previously high profits, Nokia was unable to maintain its success, as they devoted more resources to technology than to understanding consumers and trends. A poor approach and a misguided focus on the product, rather than the people who would buy it, led to their economic downfall. On top of that, Nokia's managers bet on the wrong technology and operating system for their phones at a time when Android was quickly rising to the top.

Let's take a look at the **marketing mindset** together and start to build a strong business from the bottom up.

---

[1] www.wired.com/2012/04/5-reasons-why-nokia-lost-its-handset-sales-lead-and-got-downgraded-to-junk/
www.newyorker.com/business/currency/where-nokia-went-wrong

How Can This Book Help? Is It For Me?

People start a business because they have a great idea and assume that a market of people eager to pay for their idea exists. A natural, intuitive approach always leads us to look only at ourselves – to overestimating our ideas and products. It's very easy and quite common for people to slip into such a restrictive view of our own business. The problem is assuming that just because we're excited about our idea, everyone else will be too. Commercial success depends on the usefulness of our intention for someone else. At the same time, we have to meet many different criteria that are important to the client - price, quality, scalability, testability, complexity, return on investment, and much more.

There is nothing wrong with thinking up new inventions, which only end up as prototypes in our garage or thoughts scribbled on a piece of paper. When we do something for ourselves, our opinion is the only one that matters. But in the position of an entrepreneur, we need to create value not for ourselves, but for others. In exchange for the value we provide, we make money.

Our natural way of thinking, encouraged by our ego, will always bring us back to seeing things from our own perspective. However, once we realize this fact, we can influence it to our advantage. We can home in on potential clients and create products according to the precise needs of our target market. After that, selling is simple.

If we don't engage in a marketing mindset, we set ourselves up to keep asking how to better sell our product, why no one is buying it, and why the competition is thriving while we're struggling. We will fall into searching for a miracle that will fix everything, bring success, and at the same time, confirm that everything we have done so far has been correct.

Throughout my entrepreneurial practice, I have spoken with dozens of entrepreneurs and listened carefully to their experiences. As a consultant, I enjoy hearing people's stories and following the reasons behind how and why people decide to start their own businesses. I make note of the traits common to the most successful among them, and the traits of those who continually seem to just fall short of success. The difference is evident from the first glance. The successful ones speak much more about clients and solutions. They can talk about the practical impact their products have on others.

On the other hand, those who fail tend to focus solely on themselves and their creation. They describe their product and its high quality. They ask why the market doesn't want it, or how they should sell it. Entrepreneurial forums are filled with questions of *"I have a great idea; how do I find customers?"* This approach is bad from the start, and we'll get into it more later in the book.

The book, Marketing Mindset, originated as a result of my business experience and consulting practice. I use the contents of this book daily and the advice herein is valuable both to novice entrepreneurs, and those who have already built their businesses but would like to develop them further. Useful information and examples will help even new marketers in large companies. Owners of medium-sized businesses will find inspiration for getting all their people into marketing and will see the importance of personal relationships above virtual marketing tools.

Let's get to work!

What Is The Success Rate On The Market?

The Forbes Portal published an article a few years ago stating that, according to Bloomberg, 8 out of 10 companies fail in the first 18 months. This statistic is cited frequently, but unfortunately, there is no other relevant data to confirm it. The immediate problem is what is meant by the word *fail*. Is it defined as bankruptcy, layoffs, profit loss, bad investments? This statistic seems especially pessimistic, so let's explore the actual data that is available.

I will summarize what we know based on the facts. Multi-year statistics on new and extinct US companies can be found in cited articles (2), (3), and (4). These sources show that only 50% of companies survive in the US for more than 5 years and 30% for more than 10 years.

So, is there some truth to the statistic of 8 out of 10 companies? The Pareto principle operates on the 80/20 ratio, and it applies to many fields with surprising accuracy. The corporate environment is remarkably competitive, with many people working on the same things. Failure in a business doesn't necessarily mean bankruptcy or foreclosure. It can be a poor investment: whether of money, time, or most likely some combination of the two. Can we support this statement with any real data? One decent source is the website KickStarter.com. According to their statistics (5), less than 36% of projects persuade the public and earn funding. Getting funding does not guarantee success but acts as a preliminary filter among new ideas.

Another significant area of business is online selling. Overview statistics can be found on page (6). The sum for online sales in the Czech Republic in the year 2015 is listed as over 3.5 billion USD. Of this, the largest 6 businesses account for up to 1.7 billion USD. The estimate for 2020 is around 8.5 billion USD. There are approximately 46,000 e-shops in the small market of the Czech Republic, of which 6

[2] thenextweb.com/entrepreneur/2015/02/07/8-10-statistics-totally-made/#.tnw_dYLerYZM

[3] www.sba.gov/sites/default/files/FAQ_Sept_2012.pdf

[4] www.fundera.com/blog/what-percentage-of-small-businesses-fail

[5] www.kickstarter.com/help/stats

[6] www.shoptet.cz/stav-e-commerce-v-cr-2015/

occupy over 47% of the market. Most online sales flow through the few largest online stores. Tens of thousands of small sites are fighting for the rest of the market.

The US market is much bigger with the total retail e-commerce sales of $602 billion[7] in 2019. Amazon makes 47% of it! Just a single company serves half of the market. The market share of the top 50 biggest companies is over 90%, however, there are more than 20 million e-commerce retail stores in the US.

From these numbers, we come to two conclusions. The bad news is that we have a lot of competition to contend with when trying to reach our target market. But the good news is that many businesses that are failing are making basic mistakes that can be easily fixed. By reading this book, you can avoid the typical mistakes and leap ahead of the competition.

What Are The Most Common Causes of Start-up Failure?

In business, only a small minority of ideas and projects end up with long-term success while the vast majority go nowhere at all. What are the typical reasons? Let's look at some interesting statistics from CBInsignts.com[8].

---

[7] www.digitalcommerce360.com/article/us-ecommerce-sales/
[8] www.cbinsights.com/research-reports/The-20-Reasons-Startups-Fail.pdf

The most common reason for start-up failure is simply the lack of market demand (up to 42% of projects). This number is quite high, but it comes as no surprise. As we will describe later in the book, many ideas come to the table with no connection to real-world clients. Someone gets an interesting idea and they begin developing it. They will come up with a product or service, fine-tune the details, write-up a business plan, and only then begin looking for an answer on how to sell it. In many cases, there is no answer because there is no group of consumers interested in buying it.

It is much better to start with this sentence: *"This group of people or companies is struggling with this **specific** problem and here I have a solution."* An entrepreneur with this approach is in a better position from the start and enjoys a much higher probability of success.

Among other top reasons for failure, CB Insights statistics rank: running out of money (29% of projects), not having the right team (23% of projects), and getting outcompeted (19% of projects). Also, in the top 20 reasons why, businesses crash and burn are: poor marketing, unfavorable pricing policy, unsatisfactory product quality, ignoring customers, investment disputes, and general loss of focus.

Why are we talking about the statistic of success? Right from the start, we want to point out that, in business, only a select few succeed. When we say *"succeed"*, we don't mean only making enough profit to survive but really *succeed* in the form of building a solidly growing company with stable turnover and a satisfied client base.

When we start with any new business, we should consider the fact that we must be better than most others who are attempting to develop something similar. Statistically, the odds might seem against us, but do not despair. It is not a random process–everything is in our hands. Our path to success is to devise a plan that overcomes most of the direct and indirect competition and convinces the target market that working with us is worthwhile.

This book, *Marketing Mindset*, aims to awaken your interest in business and personal development and help you build a strong foundation from the start. The themes of this book are engaging in proactive, creative thinking; cultivating a positive client-forward approach; and focusing on people over products.

After reading this book and understanding its main points, you will have an immediate advantage over the competition. Through my consulting work, I have found that the causes of failure are the same, or at least quite similar, across a variety of disciplines. In short, many entrepreneurs lack the *marketing mindset* that we will discuss in this book. As the famous businessmen say, *"Success is born in the mind"*. Let's get to work on the mind!

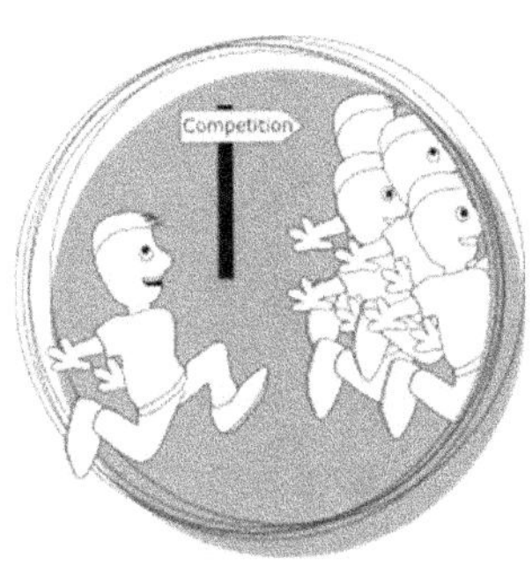

How To Succeed In Tough Competition.

As I have said before, success amid tough competition requires more than just having a good idea. You need a product that solves a specific problem for a specific group of people. Rather than trying to outsmart the competition, it's better to find or create a market in which no competition exists.

Example: A few years ago, I worked for an American company that developed software for online stores. The owner of the company took a very interesting path to business success that perfectly illustrates how to stand out from the competition.

An unbelievable number of products exist in the area of internet tools because programming doesn't require a large investment into workspace or production technologies. Even students can successfully create a functional program. For example, in the field of online shops, there are over 200 different pre-made solutions and unlimited possibilities for custom development. Plenty of solutions are free of charge or are very cheap and easily adjusted. This may lead some to the conclusion that, with so much competition, there is no point in developing another similar product.

The owner of the aforementioned company owned an online shop with spare parts and tires for cars. Since no online store really met the demand for this type of product, they were forced to develop their own solution. (The sale of spare parts for cars requires working with a large database that connects car models with suitable parts.)

Over time, they offered their new software to re-sellers of auto parts and bicycles, which brought new possibilities and significantly streamlined their business. In the auto parts business, there was almost no competition and the company slowly grew into the field of online selling. In time, they began accepting different types of contracts and increased their client base. The company continues to be successful today.

Let's consider everything that preceded this company's success as an internet store. **The first point** was a very narrow focus. They sold solutions specific to the automotive sector. Sellers of shoes, t-shirts, and electronics were not their target market. **The second point** was a thorough knowledge of the market and its needs. Since the owners of the company operated their own online shop with automotive parts, they understood exactly what problems needed to be solved. When talking with their clients, they were able to demonstrate a complete understanding of the field. This is quite different from the typical, *"We offer complex solutions in many fields"*, that many companies actually use.

Tip. Many people believe that to start a business, they must come up with some miracle idea and bring it to greatness. The only problem is that a great idea never comes. It's important to work in an industry that interests us and chat with the people in our field. If we enjoy cars, we're going to hang around mechanics, car dealers, and parts manufacturers. If we enjoy cooking, we draw inspiration from being in the kitchen. If we enjoy working with iron, we go to a blacksmith's shop to check out their decorative gates and fences. The specific area of interest doesn't matter.

Today, it's fashionable to have an academic title, even at the cost of having a low-quality education. Universities have grown rapidly, producing graduates who don't know how to use their education or find work in their field of study.

On the other side, there is always one guy you meet at a party who mounts roofs or manufactures custom trusses and says he doesn't need marketing; he doesn't even use the internet or social media networks. He does quality work with little competition. He even has customers waiting months for his services. Same with the artisanal blacksmith, who specializes in creating decorative gates and fences. He has so much work that he can't get to all his customers. He has no competition for miles. People come to him based on recommendations, without him having to do any active marketing. All this and he makes good money for his labor.

Example. For a negative example in the field of online shopping, let's look at a case from a business forum. Two novice entrepreneurs asked how others would value software for online shopping, as they had decided to develop such a product.

It's probably obvious that, with this approach, the project crashed before it even started. These naïve entrepreneurs had no useful experience in the field of online sales, no idea who their target market is, and no idea what problems they were trying to solve. The only thing that could emerge from their efforts would be some general type of shopping cart program, which wouldn't be attractive to any particular group. Moreover, amid the competition of hundreds of similar solutions, their product would be completely buried. Without a huge marketing budget, only a negligible amount of potential clients would even be aware of its existence.

There's Only One Winner. Or Is There?

Entrepreneurship, or even corporate careers, are sometimes compared to sports, with many participants competing for one gold medal. By this way of thinking, anyone who doesn't become the richest or most powerful person in the room is not considered successful. The analogy of business as a sport is inaccurate in many ways and contributes to unpleasant working conditions.

A career, whether in entrepreneurship or the corporate sphere, is not a sport with the same goal for everyone. In professional sports, thousands of athletes strive toward the same objective with only a few victors. Collectively, we only acknowledge the winners and aren't interested in athletes who don't make it to the top in their field. While sports can be inspiring, providing a driving force to spur the athlete forward through hard work and self-improvement, victory remains the only goal. If the goal isn't met, it's a big disappointment and all their hard work will have been in vain. We see the joy of winners on TV, but don't spend as much time thinking about all the athletes who didn't make it as far. However, sports have clear rules, fixed goals, and the participants know what they are getting into. Do careers work the same way?

Viewing a career like a sport distorts reality and leads to negative feelings of frustration, disappointment, and failure. Sports are built on comparing strength, ability, speed, and intelligence. However, careers do not require external comparisons. The only thing that matters is that we feel we're doing meaningful work that provides sufficient financial rewards and we enjoy doing. We don't need anything else to enjoy doing our work. If we lose the sense of meaning in our activities, no amount of monetary compensation will prevent frustration. We may continue working by rationalizing that our job keeps us fed and clothed, but motivation quickly fades. I know some incredibly successful people who have turned their lives upside down – left high positions in the corporate sphere or completely changed careers, for example, switching from management to a craft or trade.

Once we stop comparing ourselves to others, we gain a whole new sense of freedom. We create our values. We don't long for prestige, but for time to travel and experience new things. If travel and meeting new people is what we love, then the perk of a fancy company car won't bring us much in term of true value.

I rejected positions in corporations after graduating from university because my main goal is to build – companies, technology, business relationships, and my knowledge. I want to continue to develop, learn new things, and meet interesting people. These values are much more important to me than money. And I didn't mind having a cheaper car at all. I have other goals I can brag about.

Create your own set of values and goals for your life and follow through on them. If you find your work is directing you to new and unexpected places, don't worry. Acquaintances or family members may try to tell you that you're making a mistake, that you're unwisely giving up job security and taking risks. Don't take these comments to heart. Other people have no idea what values your decisions are based on; they can only comment on how they would act in your stead. It's your life and your journey to take!

Let's remember that business and careers are not like sports and there is not just one endgame. There's no single set of rules. Every company can build its own values. Target clients, business strategies, and marketing are evaluated individually. There is no necessity to be the same as everyone else in a competitive environment.

Another analogy is that business success is like a cake – there is only one and everyone on the market takes as much as they can. This is not how the market works. There is not just one cake. There is always the possibility to create a completely new market that didn't previously exist. Alternatively, you have the option to create a combination of products and services that each has plenty of competition on their own, but when provided together, are unique on the market. Imagine deciding to sell a watch – traditionally a very competitive market. You can get innovative and create a smartwatch that can operate a phone, measure heart rate, count steps, and so on. You have created a specific product that will have its own market. You can attract customers who aren't interested in classic watches and were previously never part of the market share. This creates a metaphorically untouched cake.

Luck Is Needed To Be Successful. How Much?

Bill Gross, a well-known start-up entrepreneur, gave a TED talk series on the reasons why start-ups succeed or fail. During his career, he founded dozens of companies and devoted a lot of time to the question of why some succeed, and others do not. What do his findings say?

Timing was the most important factor for 42% of start-ups that broke through. After timing were team composition (32%), the business idea itself (28%), and other factors such as business model, financing, marketing. What are the implications of timing? Is success mainly a coincidence, or can we do something to influence it?

Keep in mind that to succeed in any field, we need to understand it. Today, most fields are so complex that it's highly unlikely to get a brilliant idea in an area in which we have no experience. No matter how many long hours we spend sitting in a car, we won't get the next big idea to improve the internal combustion engine unless we are engineers with experience in the automotive industry. We also can't expect to invent a new cancer treatment without a medical background. We only really have the opportunity to improve areas that we understand intimately and in which we have reached the borders of the known and the yet undiscovered.

It's this modern complexity that makes working hard and wading through many attempts to come up with a groundbreaking idea necessary. Thomas Edison and the Wright brother, who we will discuss later in this book, spent months trying out technical solutions that didn't yield results. However, it's thanks to all their previous failures that they were able to come up with something new.

Timing a business is important, but as entrepreneurs, we can never be sure when the exact right time will come. We can predict some aspects, but it's impossible to estimate these things with precision. It's also increasingly difficult to predict the market reaction to a new product or service, especially if they are unprecedented.

Example: Text messages were limited to a very short range of characters when they first came out. This was because the creators didn't expect much public interest. The general opinion was, *"who would write out a message on their phone if they could call?"* Eventually, short messages dominated the communication market with billions of text messages sent every year.

The timing of a project is crucial, but we have a limited ability to predict all the factors. We cannot guarantee the best time choice, however, this should not discourage us from working. As the well-known saying goes: *"He who does nothing will not spoil anything."* If you do not try anything, there will be no losses or problems, but also no chance of success.

"Luck favors the prepared!" is another proverb that captures the point of this chapter. Yes, luck plays a role, but we must be prepared. Certain coincidences can have an effect on one company and not another. But it will have absolutely no effect on those who just sit around and wait for the right moment or a stroke of inspiration.

Story. On LinkedIn, I shared an article titled *"7 important things I learned in 7 years of business"*. The article received some attention and a few comments appeared. The owner of an advertising agency wrote to me personally to tell me he liked the article and identified with it. This exchange started a collaboration between us. Sometimes, a relatively small event, such as publishing an article, can attract the attention of an audience, which can later turn into a business opportunity. Many marketing activities don't have a direct business effect but can positively influence long term personal and commercial relationships.

Is Focusing Solely On Results The Right Approach?

At first glance, the title of this chapter may not even make sense, right? Results are the only things that count! In school, at work, in sports... From early in our childhood, we are taught to focus on results and that nothing else matters. Let's take a deeper look at this concept and consider if repeating a falsehood one hundred times can somehow make it true.

In the modern Western world, everything revolves around results. From primary school, we get used to being graded and evaluated only on our results. Teachers are not interested in whether getting a low grade helped you understand a topic more thoroughly or allowed you to learn something new. The grade is a classification and it goes towards your overall evaluation, regardless of how much you truly know. In mathematics, the process of solving an equation is often not evaluated at all, only the final answer. Even if you understand the process, followed the steps correctly, and made just a small numerical error, in the end, that's your own bad luck. Your answer was bad and therefore so is the evaluation of your knowledge.

Where does this approach based solely on results lead? Mostly to frustration, disappointment, and a sense of helplessness. Imagine that you are taking the time to honestly learn mathematics, you have the right approach on the test day, but bad results. You wind up with the same grade as your classmate who learned nothing. How will it affect you? Do remember having a similar feeling during your school years?

Another result of being orientated solely on results is *"the end justifies the means"*. When the process doesn't matter, only the results, we are effectively motivated to cheat. Is there any difference when you study for the exam versus just cheating? The resulting grade may not vary, despite a considerable difference in acquired knowledge. The system tells us that knowledge, progress, and learning don't matter. Some pupils even get an adrenaline rush from cheating, going so far as to invent tricks and methods to circumvent the system and get a good grade without studying the material. I knew classmates who devoted more time, energy, and creativity to circumventing the system than it would have taken to prepare honestly for exams – however, the system said that knowledge was not what was valued... At least, not as much as results.

In business, we have the advantage of being able to choose our clients and leave those that don't suit us. Sometimes the situation is more complicated, and problems arise from time to time. One of my clients commissioned a website with a complex registration system and exerted a lot of pressure on a quick finish. He regularly got upset over minor mistakes and misspellings. I always pointed out that mistakes are part of the development process and what is important is the ability to quickly address and fix problems. This is not enough for some clients. If they don't actually create anything themselves, they can't appreciate the creative process in others. Cooperation with such clients can quickly become a nightmare and not worth the effort.

So, how about those results? To get answers, we begin with a set of questions:

- Do we want to feel good about our work?

- Do we want to continually improve and feel proud of the work we have already done?

- Do we want our work to not bring so much stress, anxiety, and fear of results?

- Do we want to do away with the adage *"work first, play later"* and enjoy ourselves even while working?

If the answer is *"yes"* to these questions, then only focusing on results is completely against our interests. Why? Because emotions are fleeting, and the joy of results fades quickly. When you win the race, get the reward, and earn your money all at once, you are left with the question *"now what?"* Is the purpose of life this brief moment of delivering results? What about all the other moments? How do we perceive them and how important are they?

The slogan of a boring unfulfilled life: *"Thank God it's Friday!"*

Surely there is someone in your social network who, on Fridays, shares a photo with *"Thank God it's Friday"* and on Monday morning *"I hate Mondays"* and then goes on without making a change. Surely there is a way to live a happier life. The decision to improve your life is entirely up to you, and you can start right now—at work or in business. All it requires is adopting a positive outlook and finding the thing you enjoy and can spend your days doing.

The brief joy from results pales in comparison to the total time spent on a project. If we want to enjoy our work, we need to feel good regularly, not just at the end of a project.

Another advantage of this point of view is that, even if the project fails, we can still feel good about the work well done. Focusing on the work itself and our personal development is the key to a positive approach to business. We avoid frustration and disappointment and don't end up burning out or losing our enthusiasm for our work.

Mistakes happen and we're all familiar with Murphy's laws:

"Anything that can go wrong, will go wrong. Everything will go wrong at the worst possible moment."

We can't influence everything; we can't simply change our clients and their opinions on what we do. The one thing we have absolutely in our control is our approach. If we want to work for our own interest and not against it, it's important to continually emphasize the value of our continued labor and self-development, and not focus solely on results.

Focusing on results has one more significantly negative consequence – it disposes us to give up too soon, or worse, to cheat. If we only set high goals for ourselves, the time it takes to reach those goals will inevitably lead to growing frustration and eventually, surrender. The results-focused path is plagued with feelings of insufficiency and general negativity. A vision of the completed result is often not enough to sustain a commitment to the work at hand. Think, for example, of people's eternal efforts for weight loss. When you can't stand eating healthy food and hate to exercise, the goal of weight loss ceases to be worth it. Instead, you will find all kinds of reasons and excuses why you don't actually want to lose weight.

In my marketing practice, I have worked with clients who ended marketing campaigns even though they were successful, and I think it was the right thing to do. Unfortunately, the client set very high goals without reference to what was achievable. The campaign stopped and the client was looking for other miracle methods to fulfill their expectations. When we see only the goal in the form of numbers, sales, or new clients, we effectively block long-term growth. We don't want to admit that the path is long and challenging. Instead, we seek out shortcuts and say to ourselves *"this should be going differently"*. Success requires time and persistence. If we want to run a marathon, we have to actually run 26.2 miles and not start searching for a shortcut after a few feet.

As an independent entrepreneur who frequently works from home, I am often asked by my employed acquaintances, "how is it possible?" How can someone work from home and get things done?" Well, almost half of the time[i] spent in corporate environments is used unproductively[9]; protracted meetings, slow-moving bureaucracy, and of course, using office trifles to procrastinate getting real work done. For many employees, finding motivation in and of itself is incomprehensible. This is why I have my own business. I can balance personal freedom with work that I enjoy. Not that every task that I do is necessarily fun. I do have to address some bureaucratic tasks, but for the most part, my work is fulfilling in its technical aspects as well as in the interactions I have with clients. Ask similar entrepreneurs and they will tell you that they can't tear themselves away from their work. This is not a case of being a workaholic, as the work isn't a compensation for other things. In short, we do what we enjoy, and it brings us happiness. Making progress makes us happy.

When we implement a **marketing mindset** in our business, it will help us to define a path that will entertain and fulfill us every day. That is a happy life! To look forward to every new experience and appreciate the mistakes that push us forward. We don't procrastinate on small tasks. Progress and improvement only come as a result of addressing errors. Important knowledge in the marketing mindset is that mistakes are not our enemy, but a source of growth. The process of eliminating mistakes brings us personal development, practical experience, and make us feel good about our hard work.

---

[9] http://news.bbc.co.uk/2/hi/uk_news/4471607.stm
Why & How Your Employees are Wasting Time at Work business.salary.com/why-how-your-employees-are-wasting-time-at-work/
Facebook & Too Many Meetings The List of Employee Time-Wasters. business.salary.com/why-how-your-employees-are-wasting-time-at-work/

From childhood, it's common knowledge that mistakes are wrong and the only proper thing to do is to avoid making them. Regarding creativity and personal development, this is a destructive approach. There is an old proverb, *"only the one who does nothing, ruins nothing"*. According to my belief, avoiding mistakes is not what is important; what is important is how you approach and resolve your mistakes. I appreciate it when I see problem-solving efforts on the part of my suppliers. I would never look down on someone who acknowledges a mistake and is willing to rectify it. In fact, I greatly appreciate this approach.

And what about the results we all need?

Our work itself and the personal development associated with it are the basis of a satisfying life. If we can find joy in our work tasks, stress will cease to influence us, and we will have a productive and fulfilling life.

But what about the results that we all want so much? Of course, I do not want to minimize the importance of results. I aim only to point out the danger of looking solely at results. Complex projects and high targets require time, patience, and dedication. Only truly persistent people can succeed and bring great things to the world. A major reason why some people can persist in what they are doing is that they take joy in their own learning and progress.

Among my favorite examples are Thomas Edison and his team as they worked on developing the light bulb. They tried all kinds of materials to use for the filament of the light bulb that would shine for tens of hours, not just a few minutes. Their descriptions span over forty thousand pages – merely the documentation of materials that don't work! Eventually, however, they came to a result that changed the lives of people all over the earth.

A similar example is the Wright brothers, who built an aerodynamic chamber and continually tested various wing shapes for the possibility of flight. They spent hundreds of hours on their noble goal, all the while surrounded by the general notion that objects heavier than air simply cannot fly–yet they succeeded! On the 17th of December 1903, they became the first people to fly.

We can find countless examples in our own time. Virtually all major internet projects were preceded by multiple failures and a huge amount of work that brought no results. For example, the creators of the hugely popular mobile game *Angry Birds* previously programmed over 50 different mobile games. They were on the verge of bankruptcy and giving up – instead, they persisted and today *Angry Birds* has hundreds of millions of downloads.

Results only appear after sustained work and small steps forward. The more goals we have, the longer and more complicated the paths to completion become. **And with this, the more mistakes we have to take care of**. When our work satisfies us, we can remain on the journey to our goals for years. If we only look for a result which is not coming fast enough, we are liable to give up – our emotions compel us.

Your approach to work is your choice. Choose one that emphasizes the positive experiences along the journey, as well as satisfaction in daily work, not merely the achievement of results.

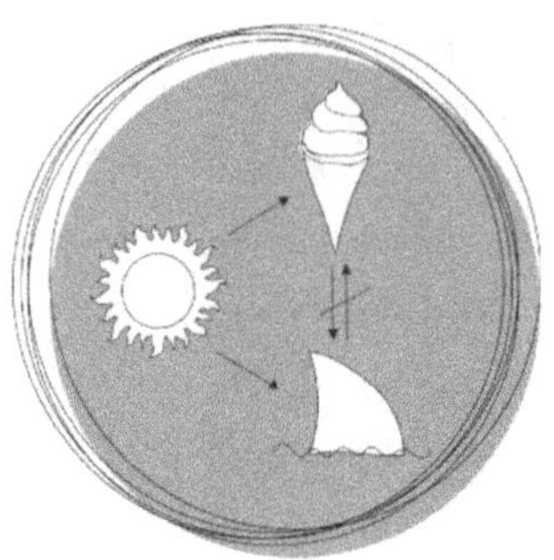

Don't Confuse Correlation With Causality

Superstition And Skinner's Pigeon Experiment

Psychologist B. F. Skinner performed an interesting experiment on pigeons, demonstrating how quickly they take on superstitions and stop perceiving causal relations between things.

The experiment went like this: the pigeons were locked in a cage and received food randomly. Over time, Skinner observed that individual pigeons began attributing the food supply to certain behaviors, which they then repeated. Some birds spun on the spot, some nodded in one corner of the cage, others lifted their head in a certain way – each pigeon seemed to believe its action would bring food.

The pigeons in the cage began to be superstitious - believing that a particular activity would bring food - and no longer investigated whether there was any causal relationship between the supply of food and their behavior. Unfortunately, many people behave similarly. Surely we're all familiar with a number of superstitions, some bizarrely ridiculous, some generally perceived. An example is the fear of the number 13. Did you know that aircraft often do not have a number 13 seat? Or that some buildings have no 13th floor – the elevator goes from the 12th right to the 14th floor. Various superstitions are based on folk traditions, religion, or just family observation.

Example. In one company, a manufacturing machine sometimes failed to work properly. The workers set a hammer next to the machine, which they would use to hit the machine in a suitable place to get it working again. When a technician offered to repair the defect, the workers asked him not to, explaining that the error was wandering around the factory. Here, they knew about it and could work around it. They believed that if they solved this particular defect, another would appear elsewhere.

Superstition is based on a misunderstanding of the difference between causality and correlation. In the next chapter, we will explain both concepts and show an example of how this ignorance manifests itself in business and the presentation of success. In *the Predictably Irrational* chapter, we look at other interesting phenomena, such as the confirmation bias, which is closely related to the misunderstanding of the relationship between correlation and causality.

Enough of The Silly Articles About Rich People's Habits

An article on LinkedIn appeared some time ago with the title *"What can Mark Zuckerberg's grey t-shirt tell us?"* It was very similar to others, such as *"10 habits of rich people," "Why the rich get up at 4 am," "15 habits of success..."* I say enough is enough!

The constant pitching of rich people's strange habits is far more annoying than motivating. I read an interesting take on this by one author, explaining that many of these so-called motivational articles are more likely to lead to depression than to success. I'm more of an evening person myself and do my best work from noon to late at night. When I'm engaged in a task, I also prefer to work at night. What should I take away from the claim that some rich people are rising at four in the morning? Should I mess with my circadian rhythm based on the vague notion that it could be the key to riches? Especially when it has no demonstrable influence on results or success?

To find the answer, we must explain **the difference between correlation and causality.** Many people confuse these two concepts and wind up in a spiral of despair. Motivational articles and quotes are everywhere, so much so that there is even a rebel group – *The world of the unsuccessful*, which has over 100,000 members. It's hard to believe that people want to be unsuccessful.

Correlation is a concept derived from statistics which merely indicates a relationship between two or more things. Correlation doesn't say that one event caused another but describes the similarity of two different processes. Sometimes correlation is the result of a cause-and-effect relationship. For example, heavy rains increase the level of water in a river. In this case, rain is the direct cause of the rising water.

It's important to note, however, that we can measure correlations for completely unrelated events. Try entering the phrase "funny correlations" into Google and see what processes exhibit the same statistical behavior. Among a few of the more amusing examples are *"Market share of Internet Explorer and the number of homicides in the USA"*, or *"Divorce rates and margarine consumption"*.

Even if there is 100% correlation between two factors, it still doesn't mean that one thing *causes* the other.

Causality addresses the causes and consequences and explains the processes leading from one to another. When we see an interesting connection drawn between two things, we must stop to ask if it's only a correlation, or if there is some causality demonstrated as well.

Back to Mark Zuckerberg's T-shirt. Does his grey shirt mean anything? Is clothing the key to fairy-tale riches? Is his choice of the t-shirt the result of something that guarantees wealth? Or does it just mean that Mark Zuckerberg is uninterested in fashion and prefers a casual look?

Likewise, with all those "Top 10" *everything imaginable about wealthy people*. While there is a certain similarity, is it a causality? Can waking up at 4 in the morning secure success, or at least help along the way? There is something positive in learning from those motivational tips and trying them out to get inspired. But let us also take care of our mental health, so that we don't take things too far and end up in frustration and rebellion. Sulking will reliably lead us only in the opposite direction of the results we would like.

Well, what about the grey t-shirt? Most likely nothing. A t-shirt is a t-shirt and work is work. Success depends on the value we bring to people. If the value we bring is large and has a strong influence on the lives of others, we will be rich. We can express ourselves however we want. We can wear a t-shirt, shorts, a suit, or even sweaters like Bill Gates. It doesn't matter.

Success Doesn't Come Overnight

Let's remember that there's no such thing as an overnight success. Success is always preceded by a large investment of time, energy, and effort towards the goal. However easily the success of others looks from the outside, we shouldn't let that fool us. Look for the talent, determination, and hard work that ensured their accomplishment. Yes, coincidence helps sometimes too, but there's a reason we have the saying, *"luck favors the prepared"*. Do you think we would have ever discovered penicillin if all Alexander Fleming had done was forget to wash a couple of bowls and find mold? Not likely.

There is a type of article that circulates social networks, giving surface-level overviews of the careers and successes of other people. If there is one thing that these articles do that drives me crazy, it's looking into the past with present-day information. Let me give you an example.

Example. In a certain article, it's written that Mark Zuckerberg invited several classmates for a meeting to discuss the idea of a social network. Those who came and joined the project are now rich–the rest were unlucky. The article points out that even those who didn't attend still had a tremendous opportunity, which they missed out on.

Where is the problem with this post? Precisely in the fact that it evaluates the past with information from the present. They didn't know how the meeting would be and had no idea what kind of impact and financial success the project would have. I think that all of us have had dozens of encounters, where all sorts of ideas were discussed.

How many of them turned out to be Facebook, Instagram, or WhatsApp?

Moreover, we have no way of evaluating if those who did come were even useful. What if one of them said: *"Enough of this meeting, let's go to the bar"*? Perhaps Facebook would never have come to be. Or maybe all of them could have been unfocused, the project wouldn't have been so great, and some other competition would have prevailed instead. Or maybe they would have decided that before creating their own platform, it would be better to join in the development of the then-popular Myspace. All of these *what-if* statements about the past have almost no informational value and do nothing at all to help us in making decisions for the future. It's far more useful to look to the past for processes that have led to concrete results. Processes are something we can research and reuse. The fact that someone either went or did not go somewhere is not a process. It's the circumstance, and circumstances are not repeating events. Let me show you an example of how circumstances can lead to new orders.

Complex Relationships Lead To Business. A Story.

One of my clients is from the United States and we have a good relationship–beyond the level of just business. This client had close friends who traveled through Europe and ended up in Prague for a few days. We exchanged contact information and met up for dinner. We had a lovely chat and found that we had many things in common. I left a good impression at the dinner, at least judging by the positive feed-back I received from my client who had put us in touch.

Over a year passed and one of the men I met at that dinner started work on a new project and wanted help with a presentation. It was our first small project. This included both a presentation, as well as some technical consultation for the project. A few months later, he got a job working for an oil company that does work in Africa. I created a special simulation program for construction logistics. That project is currently in the preparation phase and we are working on other projects together as well.

Having connections with a major oil company project raises the question of how I, of all people, managed to get a contract with applications in Africa. The answer is not straightforward, because such a contract was preceded by a complex journey of meetings, relationship-building, and a history of work and good results with various people on multiple continents. If someone wrote an article on how my business was created because I prefer working at night/wear black t-shirts/drive a black car, or what have you, it would be a non-zero correlation, but in no case will such a comparison help you to repeat the procedure.

The paths that lead to large and interesting projects are intricate and forged by relationships and contacts with new people. Motivational articles and success stories are fine as a demonstration that anything can happen, but we cannot get carried away by the paths of others. Even if they provide examples and are willing to tell us exactly *how to…*, it will most likely never lead to the same results. Very often, a person cannot fully grasp the interplay of circumstances that brought them into the position they are in today. Many things can be influenced by our actions and attitudes, but a huge part of reality is played without our intervention. How we deal with the circumstances depends only on us.

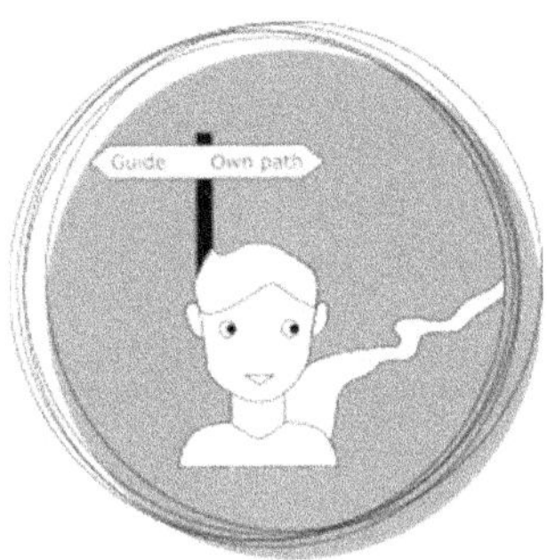

To my clients who are taken in by similar stories, I advise them to look for their way of doing things: to build businesses and relationships by themselves, to be different, original, even crazy, and unconventional. There is no one path to success and any guaranteed guides are useless. Why? Because it isn't you! Each person is different, and two people will never do things the same way. Modern marketing is about differentiating yourself, pushing boundaries, fighting myths and traditions, working with new people, and bringing value to the lives of others.

When someone tells you about their success, be more interested in their decision-making criteria and strategic principles than specific steps. One principle I use when meeting new people is to take an interest in them and offer something useful before I request something from them – give first, then ask. Another principle I follow is courteous communication under all circumstances. I recommend you define the principles that you want to define and differentiate you from your competition.

The Importance Of Explaining "*Why*"

A Missing "*Why*" Causes Chaos: A Story.

My wife and I were at a shopping mall. We were at the check-out counter with a full shopping cart when we heard a message over the PA system: "*code for staff 22, all visitors leave the building.*"

Although the announcement had a serious tone, it was an unusual situation. Some of the check-out attendees stepped away from the cash registers, leaving all the groceries where they lay on the conveyor belts. Our cashier remained seated and continued scanning items. We remained in place as well. Given the circumstances, we were unsure of how to proceed.

There was a staff member at the neighboring register. I asked him if we should really leave the building. He said yes but continued to slowly clean his place, showing no sign of panic or intention to leave.

After a few minutes, there was another message that everything was okay and that we could continue shopping. Those who had left their things went back to their shopping baskets.

The lesson of this story – **Always tell people *why*!**

The experience of the shopping center was a great demonstration of how important it is to explain *why* we have to do anything. When we say something, we may have a very clear idea of what we want to achieve, but the person we say it to may be completely confused. What else can you expect of them? This applies in all circumstances, from raising children to leading people in high positions.

Imagine the simple request *"Please clean the table"*. Clean what? What is the goal of this cleaning? Remove all the objects on the table because we want to put a tablecloth on it? Or just organize them because someone is coming over? Or get rid of any dust? Or remove the dirty plates?

In the story, a strong demand to leave the building was announced, but the *why* was not communicated. People had no idea how they should behave. Is there a fire in the building? Did someone report a bomb? An injury? Is it something in the air?

Perhaps they were attempting to prevent a panic, but the result was one of utter chaos and confusion. Moreover, at least half of the people didn't react at all, regardless of how urgent or serious the situation could have been.

Let us remember that if we don't share *why* but focus only on *what* or *how*, we risk confusing the person we are communicating with, and the results may miss our expectations by a long shot. This type of misunderstanding creates frequent conflicts in the workplace. The person dictating the task has a clear idea of what they want, but the listener creates their own image of what is expected of them based on the information given. If we don't verify that the other party understands us, the result is almost guaranteed to be different than we expected. Let's remember the axiom:

Communication is not what you say,
but what the other person understands.

"*Why*" In Marketing

Let potential clients know why they want to work for you. Are you trying to compete on price? Are you sure that price is the deciding factor for your client? Are you betting on quality? Are you sure that your clients value quality over price? Is your service complex in nature? Do potential clients understand how you can help them? Are they choosing between you and many alternative businesses?

These and all related questions need to be thoroughly considered before we begin any campaign. It's useful to know your ideal client and understand their motivation. Otherwise, any marketing efforts will have little effect other than wasting money. Later in this book, we will examine all the phases of decision making that go on during purchase and discuss at which stage it's important to explain your *why*.

Well-known American author Simon Sinek wrote some great books on the subject of "*Why*". Not only in business but also in everyday life. I fully agree with Simon's assertation that people aren't so interested in what you do, but rather *why* you are doing it. This is especially important in marketing. Regarding *what*, differentiating what you do is helpful—news, innovations, and major improvements help marketers, but they aren't enough in the long term. Patents and trademarks work only to a certain extent, and the risk from the competition is significant. A presentation missing *why* will quickly face rising marketing costs.

How to create your *why*?

For many, this is a difficult question for which they have no answer. If you are in this position, it's very likely that you're doing something different from what you would like to be doing. People who work solely for money and out of necessity likely don't have the best relationship with their work and aren't completely happy in life. Even if other aspects of life are very fulfilling, such as family, friendships, and health, people still spend much of their time working and it should bring joy. Life situations may have brought us to our current state, and maybe it won't be easy to change it. A successful person is one who is committed to making changes to seek out happiness in life.

Whatever our starting position, let's ask ourselves, what are we passionate about, what fulfills us, and in what field can we see our vocation. Try writing out these points on paper and don't limit yourself to your existing circumstances. Get creative and revive your old dreams and goals. What kind of work are you naturally attracted to? Technology? Art? People? Children? Business? Travel? Social events? Sports? Choose your path and step forward!

If we turn to what we're passionate about, then we have discovered our *why*. Your passion is your *why*. When we know what we want to do, we also find a specialization that allows us to give value to other people. Only in this way will we earn money. It bears saying again: do not limit yourself by dismissing options just because *"that could never happen"*.

 **Example**. Do you like traveling, but it seems like you spend more money than you make? Engage your creativity! Why not

try making a video blog, tutorials, or tips for travelers? Once you build a sufficient fan base, this can be an effective commercial opportunity. Once we match our hobbies with the habit of marketing mindset and listening to people, suddenly countless possibilities and ideas for businesses appear. For example, you can be a tour guide for a few little-known monuments that tourists rarely get to. Create something unique in the field of travel that has no competition.

We can find hundreds of similar examples. I know many talented people who started just like this. They had a regular job, but their passions were elsewhere. At some point, their hard work and effort returned in the form of interest in their services. They were able to leave their jobs and become independent entrepreneurs. Most are not well-known wealthy entrepreneurs, but it doesn't matter. They do good work, provide a quality service to their clients, and above all, live happy lives with vocations they enjoy.

The goal of a marketing mindset is not just selling. The much deeper idea is to find a job and a lifestyle that will fulfill us every day. We all have our dreams. Let's start standing behind them.

Popular Business Concepts How To Understand Them

When talking to entrepreneurs or people who have an interesting idea but don't know where to start, I begin by asking them for details about their idea. In many cases, there is evident naivety about their venture. The most common manifestation of this is a focus on their product and making adjustments to it. The creator continually tries to improve their product, all the while remaining unnoticed by their target market. Only after all of this work, do they stop to ask, *"How can I sell this?"* Having waited too long to ask this question, they will start looking at the masses of "guaranteed" instructions for success. There is a veritable sea of popular solutions, which can become treacherous to navigate. Let's look at some of the most popular among start-ups.

Popular Business Questions

Psychologists and personal coaches will tell you that the way to succeed is to ask the right questions. When we ask the wrong questions, even having the rights answers won't help us. What do these questions look like for start-up businesses? What are the most frequently asked questions?

- How do I create my brand?

- Can you help me create a brand?

- How much should I invest in my new brand?

- How can I find an investor?

- How can I create viral content to get attention?

These are questions that contain some modern buzzwords which can be difficult to comprehend or mean something other than what the novice entrepreneur understands.

We are bombarded on all sides by different fashionable concepts that we don't necessarily understand, but we feel pressured into incorporating them into our new business. We end up spending a lot of time and money on inefficient endeavors. Let's take a closer look at some of them.

What Is A Brand?

The typical layperson's definition of a brand is some name or logo that performs sales and marketing miracles. This is far from reality.

A brand by itself doesn't mean anything. The important thing is what the brand represents. Nike is not merely a check-shaped logo, Apple is more than just phones and computers with partially eaten fruit on them, Gucci means something other than handbags and accessories with a shiny "G".

What do brands mean to us and what makes brands famous? Brands are always associated with some story, history, experience, positive feelings, or exceptional service. Brands are not built in a day!

- What is Gucci? It is an expression of luxury and style. After that, it makes quality goods.

- What is Ferrari? Not just sports cars. It is a lifestyle: speed, freedom, and expression using the famous and enviable brand. Some Ferrari car models are sold out a few days after the announcement of a new line. Owners can feel like elite members of society. They attract attention and interest on the road.

- What is Nike? Not just clothes and shoes! Nike with their slogan *Just do it* inspires people to overcome their limits and is associated with motivation, success, and world-class athletes. At times it's not even clear from their ads what exactly they're selling. The company knows that their product matters less than the story and emotions that they are selling with it.

- ◆ What is Apple? It's more than just computers and electronics. Apple is the embodiment of the American dream. It's the story of a company that started in a garage and conquered the market in the field of technology. Apple is all about progress, innovation, and brand loyalty.

These well-known brands illustrate how the tangible product is not really what the customer is buying. It's the story, the image, the feeling of belonging to a group, and getting to show it to the world. People have an innate need to belong and are willing to spend money to find that feeling. The physical product doesn't matter all that much

The story must be based on the values **we** believe–whatever makes **us** unique and interesting. We need to bring something to the table that our clients align with. A product or service alone is not enough.

Moreover, the product or service itself is often easily reproduced and can be sold under some other brand name. There are no major differences between shoes, clothes, televisions, or mobile phones. Similar quality and prices exist across competing brands. How should the client decide? And from our side, how can we create a product that, even if copied, will fail to do as well as when it's sold by our company?

The short answer to these questions is in those previously mentioned buzzwords: story, originality, emotions, humanity, feelings of success, the feeling of belonging to a group that shares our values, and the feeling of being unique and important. This is immensely important for new projects to establish, but many people ignore them as seeming too vague or esoteric to have real relevance.

Many entrepreneurs will focus exclusively on the technical side of the project: What the characteristics of the product are, what features it will have, how it will be packaged, where it will be sold, how much it will cost, and so on. I have met many businessmen who just describe the technical side of their product in detail. I once saw a business plan like this that spanned more than 100 pages! Incredibly, not once was there an answer to the question **"What will our company do better?"** or *"Why will clients chose this product over the hundreds of similar ones on the market?"*

The absence of a marketing mindset and focusing only on the product output has several implications. When a creator is looking only at their product, they might get the feeling that their product will work for everyone. While this may be true, it's impossible to market to everyone. They might say *"just market it to anyone"*. In reality, this manifests itself as *"marketing for no one"*. Conversions will be low. People may come to the website, take a look, maybe even say *"oh, that's nice!"* and then leave. Marketing will become more and more expensive and the return on investment (ROI[10]) will be negative. Fixing this isn't worth the endless cycle of optimizing the marketing campaign and trying new tricks. Positive changes only occur after the application of a new and better approach.

---

[10] ROI – return on investment

What Is A Business Plan? Do I Need One?

The business plan is another modern concept that everyone has heard of. It should be a summary of working tasks, predictions, and information that will lead to the startup and development of a new business. We might be able to agree upon that definition. Exactly what information should be there is the topic of lengthy discussion.

Even an extensive business plan may not lead to success

That previously mentioned, extensive, hundred-page business plan for an internet project was carried out with a spirit of optimism, probably resulting from the size of their potential market. The plan contained all sorts of figures about the number of small firms, tradesmen, and independent contractors needed. It also featured different demographics and development predictions. It all looked very nice—it even contained sophisticated graphics and visual aids. Where is the big **BUT**?

BUT the business plan had no **SWOT** analysis (analysis of Strengths/Weaknesses and Opportunities/Threats), and no thoughts about prospective clients or analysis of competitors. There was no mention of the target market's needs, what the competition was, or even what they could bring to potential customers. Most of the work that went into the business plan was useless because it didn't contain a shred of useful data.

When the product was placed on the Czech market, it only had a minimal response in the form of free trials, but no paying customers. Despite expectations set by the business plan, it didn't get discovered. Even those who tried the product with a free trial ended up not buying it.

It would have been enough to look at the forums for business owners and compare competing products. It would be clear that the tool described in the business plan was very nice but lacked key functions for customers in the Czech market.

In his book, *The Startup Owner's Manual,* Steve Blank takes the view that for a novice entrepreneur, the best thing is just to start doing SOMETHING. More important than writing out comprehensive business plans is to get out into your target market and find out what problems need solving.

Steve Blank describes the story of a giant start-up project with a large budget that ended in a fiasco. The project was too *internally focused*: building structures and creating increased growth and development for the company itself. They forgot to consider what the target market needed and what it would be willing to pay for. Despite the unlimited budget and the involvement of top managers, the project collapsed.

One way to start a new project is to invent a *Minimum Viable Product*. The aim is to create the first product at a low cost and to market it as quickly as possible. All other enhancements will then stem from the experience of real users. This avoids spending time implementing creative improvements that won't be valued by the market. Moreover, if the product has no chance to succeed, the lesson is learned quickly, and additional resources aren't wasted.

The pitfalls of a lengthy business plan

To name a few:

- We don't have our own relevant and reliable data yet.

- Our plan will mainly be a set of hypotheses.

- We might use incorrect assumptions at the start and thus draw useless conclusions.

- We focus on information and figures that support our beliefs. We don't like to admit facts that don't correspond to them. We aren't critical enough of ourselves.

- We are inspired by superficial stories about the success of others, although we don't know the complex connections and circumstances behind them.

- We are inspired by large companies, but start-up companies are completely different from established corporations.

I could expand on this list for many more pages, but the question at hand is how to deal with these pitfalls and get to starting a business? The short answer is *communication* and *listening*. The absolute foundation is to know *why* and *for whom* you want to work. Who are the clients and what problems need addressing? The long answer is, well...this entire book.

How To Create Viral Content?

Viral means content that spreads itself, without extensive advertising activity of the creator–whether it's a video, article, photo, or song. Creating something viral is the dream of every marketer. Why? All entrepreneurs want their work to be shared by private individuals for free. While others pay for extensive advertising campaigns, viral content spreads itself.

Without exception, my clients ask if I can create viral content for them. The question alone is not very good. The rule here is that ***content becomes viral.*** What does that mean? Virality depends on more than just the creator alone. We can do our utmost to spread content across all possible networks, but the result can still be vague disinterest from our audience.

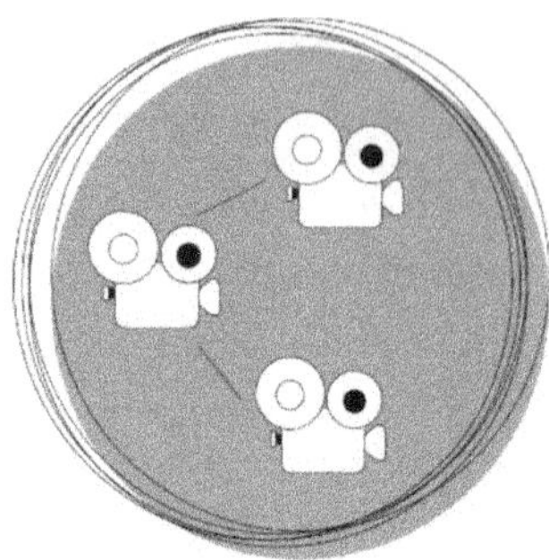

The fact that it is the *content* that becomes viral is a crucial aspect of our approach. When we create something great for ourselves, there is no guarantee that a wider audience will feel the same way. For something to become viral, it needs to appeal to a wide audience. When faced with the goal of creating viral content, we need to be clear about the type of potential we have. Let's summarize a few essential points:

♦ All viral videos, articles, or songs create strong emotions in the consumer.

♦ Emotion, emotion, emotion...This is so important for viral content that even writing it three times isn't enough. Plainly stating facts or emphasizing expert knowledge won't capture the masses.

♦ What emotion is the target of our content? Joy, sadness, pride, hope, compassion, and fear all work well.

♦ Viral content will divide the audience. It's impossible to create something that will be fully liked by everyone. People like to argue, denounce different opinions, and defend their attitudes and worldviews. It's important to exploit this phenomenon.

♦ Viral content benefits from the activity of fans as well as critics. If it doesn't generate discussion, it won't be seen widely. Social networks are programmed to support posts with high user activity (likes, comments, and shares).

How to increase the chance of creating something viral

We have established that *content* is what becomes viral. No one can guarantee that something they make will go viral, but we can at least increase the chances. Above are listed some of the essential aspects of viral content.

Before we prepare our content, we should first decide which emotion is going to be central to getting people to share it. Then we can get to work, carefully crafting our content so the feeling is communicated. For example, if we want to communicate a message of hope and success, we can find successful personalities or groups that have succeeded against strong odds. Or perhaps we can show success through an interesting and inspirational journey. If we want to achieve virality on our own, the story must already exist, or we need to use our creative capacity to come up with it. Authenticity goes a long way in this regard, but we can play up different aspects according to our needs.

The next step is to consider whether the resulting content is controversial enough to attract a large viewing audience. If so, that's a huge advantage. There are plenty of controversial themes; just be creative and look to the world around you. For example, we can associate our product with a member of a minority and point out how it helped them succeed in the face of prejudice and adversity. Just the presence of a minority member is often enough to arouse the interest of someone wanting to argue about their merit, and so we have created a discussion and a reason to share.

Among the most often-shared viral content are videos featuring cute animals or small children. If it works for your product, consider using this theme. Other popular categories are controversial topics such as political opinions, immigration, race, sexual orientation, and so on. It must be said that with these topics, we're always on thin ice and it's easy to cross one imaginary boundary or another. Results can wind up generating a lot of negativity surrounding our brand or even put us at odds with the law. Still, these topics work and are widely used. Each person must look to their morals to guide them in this. Let me give you an example.

Example. Recently, leaflets of a supermarket[11] were distributed featuring models with dark skin tones. Automatically this generated discussion. On one side were those who are intolerant of different races, and on the other side, advocates of tolerance. We can certainly philosophize about the moral correctness of exploiting this theme for attention, but as marketers, the conclusion is that the campaign did its job extremely effectively. Some people defended one way of thinking, the others defended the opposite. In either case, the result was a flurry of activity on social media and the extensive sharing

---

[11] Many countries are homogenous and the questions of race always resonate in the society.

of posts containing the name of the business chain...And completely for free. If the controversy gets big enough, the mainstream media will begin to cover it. Journalists are required to obtain information from both parties. Suddenly the string of events has presented the opportunity to make comments in the media and gain even more visibility for free. Comparable visibility through advertising alone would come at the cost of thousands of dollars.

I recommend using positive themes and promoting happy emotions in campaigns. Each of us must make our own choices.

Watch out for the unwanted consequences of virality

- Although creating viral content is akin to an Olympic event for marketers, we should consider some of the downsides. Content that is shared a lot will attract its share of anti-fans—or in slang, *haters*. While this group is essential for the virality to occur, they can exert a strong negative social impact on the content's creator. Expect the circulation of fake information, ugly rumors, accusations of fraud, or manipulation of results, and so on. We'll meet the *"fact-checkers"* everywhere. In a short time, someone starring in a YouTube video can attain celebrity status and completely lose their privacy. The speed at which information is disseminated across modern media outlets means all of this happens very fast. All participants in the creation of something potentially viral should consider the consequences in advance and agree that they're prepared to take the risk. The internet doesn't forget, and once content goes up, it can stay online forever.

Don't Be Pulled Down By The Crowd

These concepts that we've heard about over and over need to be understood and implemented in business. A large portion of the population follows fashion and keeps up with mainstream trends. However, thinking like the majority may do more harm than good. In the introduction, I stated that a minority – a clever group of people who do things differently than others – succeed in business. Big investors might try to tell us which way the market is going according to their strategy, only for the market to go in the exact opposite direction. And the result is obvious – how many investors will equal Warren Buffet, even though millions of people try their luck on the stock market?

The crowd effect, modernity, a desire to not be different or stand out too much: these cause people a lot of lost opportunities and bad decisions. The crowd effect can be exploited in two ways – positively (by giving value) or negatively (by spreading bad information).

Let's look at an example from history that illustrates the crowd effect and how it can be used.

The Klondike Gold Rush

In August 1896, American gold miner George Carmack discovered gold in the remote Canadian region of Klondike. News of this finding spread quickly and attracted more aspiring gold miners to the area.

Information spread much slower in those days, so news of the gold didn't reach America until the following year. In that time, the amount of gold in Klondike waned and plots of land had been bought up. The gold fever broke out in San Francisco, and tens of thousands of people made their way north. These people gave up their jobs, bought supplies, and set out to make their fortunes.

Many individuals traveled for more than a year. Klondike is a region in the north of Canada, made impassable due to snow and ice for much of the year. Temperatures there drop below -58°F (-50°C). To make matters more complicated, the Canadian government regulated a minimum amount of inventory. People had to transfer hundreds of kilograms. They had to split them into smaller bags weighing about 30 kg each. After transferring one package, they had to return and carry the next. The route from the gold deposits to the ports – thousands of miles one-way – had to be trekked multiple times back and forth. The trip for Americans traveling to Klondike lasted more than a year, and many perished along the way.

The road to gold was misery, and only a few of those who started were able to overcome all the obstacles. Still, thousands of gold miners arrived in Klondike only to be met with disappointment. By now, almost two years had passed since the initial discovery of gold. Most of the gold had already been excavated and the land all bought up. Newcomers found work in mines or unsuccessfully searched for remnants of gold on their own.

The crowd effect works similarly even today. The result is that most people take a loss or end up disappointed. When the crowd starts paying attention to a business opportunity, it's usually already too late. The exception to this would have to be some innovation that fundamentally changes the whole sector, but this requires extraordinary effort, insight, and luck.

We can see that joining the crowd is a risk with a predictably poor outcome. But there are other opportunities that we can profit from by using the crowd effect. The principles that were valid a century ago hold up today. How so? Klondike had some admirable personalities.

A certain gold miner, Joseph Laude, arrived at Klondike. He quickly understood that it was already too late to look for gold. Instead, he thought about a way to use the crowds of gold miners as a business opportunity. He had a great idea! He bought over 178 acres (72 hectares) of land and began building a city to house the thousands of new people that continued to arrive. He sold parcels for houses and set up shops and even a saloon. He named the town after geologist G. M. Dawson, and it's known even today as Dawson City.

Over one hundred thousand people came from the United States to Klondike. Tens of thousands of them arrived at their destination only to find disappointment and subsequent poverty. Yet Laude arrived and understood that the real gold was not in the ground, but the business-opportunity created by the crowds, and built not only wealth but a whole new city.

Are there any modern equivalents of the Gold Rush? Yes! One of them is Amazon Business. Resourceful entrepreneurs offer a variety of courses on this platform, even though it's demanding and risky investment. The number of ads offering courses gives the impression that Amazon Business is a modern way to get rich quick. Unfortunately, if you're reading this now, it's already too late. Sellers on Amazon are in the millions at this point, and usually, products can be purchased directly from the manufacturers through Amazon anyway. Additionally, almost everything consumers could want is on Amazon in direct competition with other retailers. Amazon Business hasn't been a lucrative endeavor for several years now and is only becoming more challenging and less profitable. For many companies, it serves only as advertising without bringing much of an economic yield. The target has changed from *generate a profit through sales* to *be seen and build recognition.*

One of my clients got sucked into the promise of Amazon Business, completed a course at a cost of several thousand dollars, and then was confronted by the reality of the situation. They couldn't sell their products amid the huge volume of competitors and ended up sinking several thousand more dollars into the endeavor. This was a very expensive learning experience for my client, but great for the seller of Amazon Business courses.

Another modern equivalent of the gold rush is trading on the stock market – shares, bonds, funds, forex. When it comes to investing, typically only big players thrive–those with access to non-public information and with large teams of analysts at their disposal. Brokerage firms, which make accessing the stock market possible for the public, earn fees, or a percentage on each transaction. The more people trading, the better! The stock exchange is easily accessible to anyone with an interest in it.

The vision of easy earnings on the stock market is supported by various business advisors. On the internet are thousands of books and videos about trading shares that promise riches. The question remains: If the authors of these publications make so much money on the stock exchange, why are they spending their time writing books or creating videos that make comparatively very little money? The answer is that most of them are doing better selling their advice about the stock market than they are in the market itself. To make an analogy with Klondike: those who have not found gold themselves provide services to others on how to look for it.

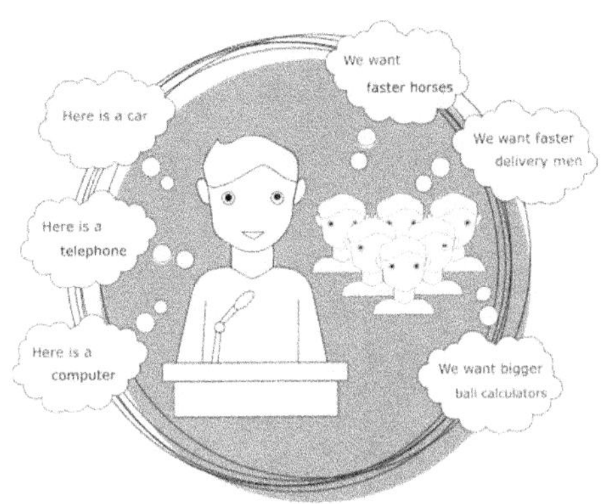

Do Customers Know What They Want?

Customers don't even know what they want unless you show them. Or do they?

This is an idea made popular by Steve Jobs in marketing for Apple. Until recently, I didn't pay much attention to this method. Then one client told me she didn't like surveys because the people surveyed rarely knew what they wanted. She gave an example of asking people 200 years ago how they would like transportation improved – they probably would have said faster horses.

Suddenly Steve Jobs' method began to make sense to me. I always invite my clients to be actively interested in their customers. Otherwise, they end up inventing things that no one wants to buy and end up with the question *"how do I sell this?"* By this time, it's already too late. Business miracles are not a common occurrence.

Should You Ask The Market What They Want Or Not?

How should it go? Should you ask your target market what they want? Or should you not bother because they probably don't even know in the first place? From the perspective of a practicing marketer with hundreds of hours with clients, I have some practical advice.

The truth lies somewhere in the middle. It doesn't help much to simply ask your market what product or service they would like. They probably don't know unless you provide some potential solutions. If they knew, someone would have already taken to producing the solution. Coming up with solutions is up to us and our own creativity.

Customers may not have the solution, but know what they want fixed

The customer doesn't need to know the solution to know exactly what problem they want fixed. If we, the entrepreneurs, don't take this into account, then our solution can completely miss the needs of our clients. Our product can be technologically advanced and of great quality, yet still not be suitable for any group of clients. If this is the case, the product will be problematic and costly to sell. Most small businesses don't have the capital to push such products to the market with massive advertising. Even large companies have experience with the unsuccessful "push" method of marketing.

Focusing on the product condemns a company to failure, no matter how big it is

In his book, Simon Sinek raises the question of why big train companies at the end of the 19th century didn't invest in air travel, which was a breakthrough at the time. This is a great question. Instead, they left the future of transportation untouched and many eventually went bankrupt or were bought out.

Why did this happen? The answer is simple. These companies focused exclusively on *train* transport, rather than focusing on passenger transport. If they had, they surely would have noticed the growing interest in air travel. Even large successful companies have this problem of focusing only on their product rather than the greater service they should provide. Train travel was no exception. They asked their customers how to make train travel better. But the customers wanted what the train companies could not yet provide – speed over great distances.

This is essentially what Steve Jobs was talking about. Customers didn't know that they wanted an iPod. It doesn't matter to them what the product is. That is why Apple didn't ask how it could improve the

Walkman. Apple sold the concept of having 1000 songs in your pocket – the exact technological solution was irrelevant. Other companies sold MP3 players with 16 GB of memory and radio. At first glance, this is a fundamentally different approach to marketing.

Communicating With Clients Through Marketing

One of the most important factors in marketing communication is a genuine interest in clients and their problems. Not just at a surface level, but on a personal level as well. How do they feel when using your product? Or how would they like to feel? What kind of experience do they want to be having? What problems do they want to solve? What options have been considered up till now?

We don't want to make our clients do our job for us. For example, when we ask how they would better address web traffic on their site, we may get an answer that makes no sense from a technical point of view. People don't want or need to understand everything–they have enough to worry about already. When speaking with them, we should strive to see things from their perspective as much as possible. For example: what is upsetting or frustrating about the internet? Is it something they need fixed right away, so they can have time for their more important tasks? Which options were considered or tried out? Once this issue is solved, how will their day be improved? What would make them happier? Where does their inner inspiration come from?

When we don't communicate with our clients, we might get overly creative and invent solutions "on their behalf." The trouble arises when we create a solution to a problem we don't fully understand. When we don't have enough information, we begin to use fragments from various sources. This creates an attempted *one product fits all* solution, which usually proves to be *one product fits none* solution. Overvaluing our knowledge and perspective will lead us to creating a product that doesn't adequately suit any segment of the market. There is no o*ne product fits all.*

For example, it may not always be advantageous to add new (albeit cool) features to devices or software. Your website or device may end up so complicated that it turns potential clients off from using it, and you may end up seeing a radical spike in customer support inquiries.

Example. Telephone manufacturers compete in terms of their devices' hardware parameters, while most customers neither understand nor care about these things. As performance levels and speeds gradually saturate, manufacturers look for ideas to attract customers away from their competition. It becomes very complex because all phones are basically the same.

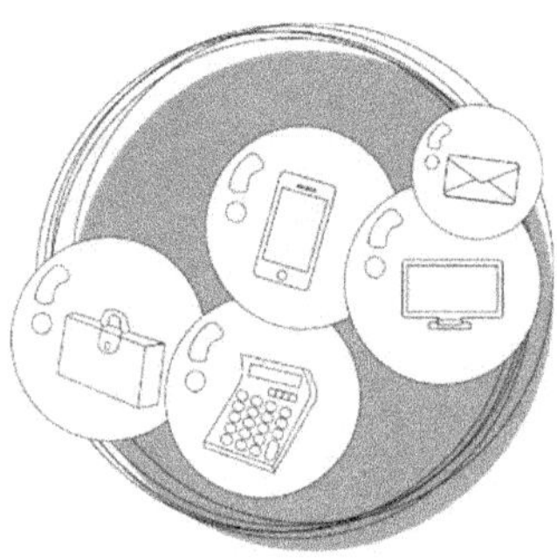

Among the competition in the mobile phone market, companies have managed to secure success by offering all kinds of small personal touches for their phones: Stickers, cases, sleeves, anything customizable. Why? Because they know that all phones are almost identical, yet being different is important to young consumers. The phone itself doesn't entice the consumer, but a slap on a curated selection of customizable beautification options, and you have the market's attention.

Successful selling is ensured by in-depth knowledge of the market. Who are the clients and what problems are being addressed? How do they communicate, how do they shop, what are their preferences?

Are they technologically proficient or laymen? What kinds of options do they have via our direct and indirect competition?

 Get interested and find out. It's better to spend one hour with a potential client than 10 hours sitting in an office brainstorming.

Example. We've already mentioned what you should avoid in marketing: the *one size fits all* approach. No matter how universal our product may be, it cannot serve everyone. Even if it could, running multiple marketing campaigns to cover all potential users simply isn't possible.

This way of thinking can be prevalent in services which are rendered to diverse groups of clients–financial advisors, nutritionists, coaches. Perhaps the coaching principle is the same for business executives, individuals seeking self-improvement, and professional athletes. A coach may have the feeling that one method can work for everyone. But even if this were the case, it still wouldn't be effective to market to everyone.

In my practice, I have met coaches who presented their services online as "suitable for anyone." They tried to reach out to diverse market shares – business executives, private individuals, married couples, new entrepreneurs, and the like. For each corner of the market, they tried a marketing campaign, which almost universally resulted in little success. At the bottom of the list of all their services, they mention that they also coach athletes. *Now there is a potential specialization!* Athletes have special needs and only want to work with a coach who will understand them.. Once a coach moves into a specialization, *"soccer coach"* for example, the competition decreases drastically. Potential clients can now be found, marketed to, and connected to the services they want.

The ideal result of a marketing mindset is to reduce the competition to a minimum. Specialization in a narrow field will help you to distinguish yourself from others while developing your expertise to a higher level. People and businesses prefer suppliers with industry knowledge because they are easier to communicate with. When you coach sports, you're in a better position to help athletes than a generic coach. Athletes know that you understand them. If you do programming within the financial sector, you're much more likely to get a contract in that field compared to a generalized software company.

Don't be afraid of the feeling that you're leaving opportunities on the table. It isn't a loss, but a benefit. Building expertise and a specific combination of abilities will make your brand unique.

A Little Marketing Theory And Its Evolution

What Is A Marketing Mix?

The formal concept of a marketing mix dates to the 1940s. The principle it describes, however, has been used for thousands of years. In this chapter, I will explain how to use these marketing mix models, and how and why they have changed over the last century.

Marketing mixes are more than just a theoretical model. They are connected to real-world work and campaigns, as well as fundamental perceptions of business and entrepreneurship. Knowing each mix will show us how to think about marketing in different ways. We will learn that the most intuitive model is in fact, the least efficient–at least in today's world.

The 4P Marketing Mix

Marketing mix **4P**, or the extended version **7P**, is an intuitive approach to sales and markets. It places the product first, and the manufacturer and everything else revolves around it.

4P is derived from 4 words:

- Product

- Price

- Promotion

- Place

Additions to the 7P model include:

- **Physical** – a place where buyers and sellers can meet

- **People** – interactions between buyers and sellers

- **Process** – the mechanisms behind sales and delivery

You should note that the 4P mix includes only the seller's side; the client is not considered in this concept. It took decades before additional approaches to marketing were described. 4P is theoretically interesting and essential knowledge to have, but not enough to get by in today's marketing world.

Moving on from 4P, I will briefly describe other marketing mixes. We will consider why new marketing mixes evolved and how to apply them.

The 4C Marketing Mix

The **4C** concept originated in the 90s. Each letter stands for one of the following:

- Consumer/Customer

- Communication

- Cost

- Convenience

Marketing mix 4C is client orientated. **Product** ceases to be as important and instead the customer steps into the spotlight. Goods and services rendered can be customized if we know the client and their expectations. On the other side, buyers have more opportunities, which they are reluctant to give up by buying from only one source.

Price changes to cost, both in terms of capital and time. When ordering a product online, consumers are willing to pay more for home delivery or to a post office than for cheap transport to an inconvenient location.

Promotion changes to communication. Plastering billboards and handing out flyers with product descriptions doesn't do much. Today's market requires active communication with clients and potential buyers.

Place changes to convenience. It's not enough to provide individual delivery, but also a concrete time and method of delivery. In this new model, the seller adapts to the client, not the other way around. Why? Because the client can easily shop somewhere else.

Mix 4C is also called the *Compass Model* in the extended version **7C**. When you type the model name into a search engine, you will see a typical image of this model in the form of a compass. In the middle is Corporation/Competition and the other elements of the model (corporation, channel, commodity, cost, communication, consumer, circumstances) surround it. Although the 4C model is correctly focused on the client, in the Compass Model the focus returns to the seller. The client is no longer in the middle, rather they are just one of the many elements.

The SIVA Marketing Mix

The **SIVA** marketing mix best describes the requirements of entrepreneurship in the 21st century. The letters stand for:

- Solution
- Information
- Value
- Access

SIVA takes the concept of focusing on the client to the next level, moving completely away from the product to emphasize the solution. Every entrepreneur is quite proud of their service or product. The truth is that the client has little interest in what we are selling. **What is so important**, if not the product? It's the **solution**! The client needs to find a solution to a situation, rid themselves of some problem, or create something new.

One-way promotion is extremely inefficient and expensive. In the 4C mix, mutual communication has an important role. Its importance also applies in the SIVA model. In the SIVA model, we delve even deeper into communication. Exactly what the client needs is useful and valuable information. With the expansion of the internet and the wider availability of knowledge, the client can make a more informed choice than ever. The role of the retailer is to provide information which is interesting to the client and will help them make their decision. All necessary knowledge is obtained through communication and active interest in the needs of the target customer.

Price and cost are more complex in the SIVA model. The decision to buy or not to buy is dependent on the **perceived value**. Read that sentence one more time and save it in your memory. It's not the price that matters but the perception of the value received. This is a universal principle that applies across disciplines. Think of how many times you have turned down something free. How is that possible?! Many are shocked; "but it was *free...*". Yet they are equally uninterested. Why? Because the perceived value may be nothing at all or even negative. For example, perhaps a free flyer doesn't interest you, and taking it means you have to carry it around in your hand until you find a place to throw it away. Free food may also not be all that tempting, especially if there are health or hygiene concerns. Free software downloads take time and run the risk of infecting your computer with a virus. In every case, entrepreneurs must consider the specific factors that influence the behavior and decision making of their clients.

If you are unable to create real value for your customers, even a $0 price tag is not going to sell it. On the other hand, when we create something unique and valuable, a satisfied customer will happily pay a higher price. Just look at super luxury cars with prices in the millions. "That much money for a *car?*", you may say. But Ferrari and Rolls-Royce know that they aren't selling just any car. Their market is nowhere near that of a Honda Fit or Ford Fiesta.

The last letter in SIVA is **A** – Access. In this section, we will focus on the process of how, when, and where the client can obtain our goods and services. If your customer is employed, but your shop closes at 5:00 pm, you lose potential sales. Expensive or inconvenient forms of delivery deter customers from a product, even at a favorable price.

If you provide home delivery for your product, you may limit yourself to one carrier, and discourage any customer who has had a bad experience with that carrier before. I, for example, prefer not to use the services of the USPS, as I had a bad experience I don't wish to repeat. If the commercial carrier is a dollar or two more expensive, I don't mind. If I see only one delivery option, I shop somewhere else. The good price or available discounts no longer matter because, in addition to the money paid, I need to spend additional time to actually get my hands on the goods.

It's not only product delivery, but also access to information. If the customer can't find contact info on the website, or the page loads slowly, or looks suspicious or chaotic in some way, they will shop elsewhere. We live fast, but also shop fast and quickly make up our minds to leave a website or store we don't like or where we can't find what we're looking for.

 **Example**. Some books suggest you *"go directly from 4P to SIVA"*. Let me give an example of what that means.

When driving around, you will sometimes come across empty billboards with *"advertising space"*, or *"billboard for rent"*, or some other phrase written on them. This is 4P at work because it's just describing what is for sale. No thought is given to the needs of the client. The advertisement doesn't pack much power. How could they use SIVA instead? Recently I saw a nice example. The following was written on one empty billboard:

"Your customers are spending the same amount of time looking here as you are."

This is a better example of advertising. What are people who buy billboard space looking for? They want their poster to be seen – for as much time as possible. That is exactly what that phrase represents. It isn't just about the advertisement space, but also the *time spent looking* that is provided by the good location of the billboard in question.

Look at your promotional materials. What is more prominent? Your product, or the value you provide to your customers? Remember, these two things are not the same!

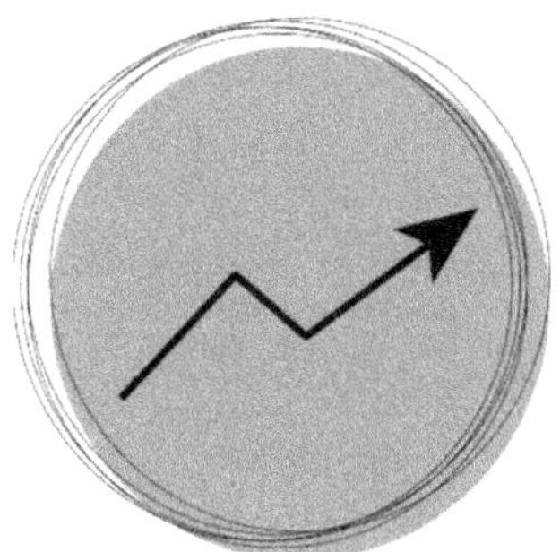

The Inevitable Advancement of Marketing Mixes

Marketing mixes and their development is quite an interesting topic for understanding modern marketing and basic rules. The 4P-type marketing mix has worked for centuries. It was formally described in the mid-20th century, later to become the basis of marketing theory for another 50 years. More modern approaches, such as SIVA, were created in the 90s as a result of technological and societal changes.

Why were these changes inevitable? The answer is two words: **competition** and **technology**. Centuries ago, there was far less competition than there is now. Information wasn't readily available, and most people only had basic education. Craftsmen were esteemed and their work was highly valued: blacksmiths, tailors, cobblers, and the like. They handed down their craft to their children and apprentices. There were significantly fewer people alive and the population density was much lower. In those days, you would have to travel to another village or even farther to run into another craftsman of the same trade.

The technology was limited, and production was slow and largely dependent on manual labor.

For self-employed craftsmen with more work than they could manage, this set-up was advantageous. Price could be manipulated and the product itself was of utmost importance. When customers wanted or needed something, they sought it out – no marketing necessary. When you made shoes, quality and price were crucial. Clients would travel tens of miles for quality shoes. Product, price, and place of the sale were the core elements of your business and marketing. Even markets and fairs didn't create as much competition as there is today. A few producers of shoes, clothing, or cookware found ways to distinguish themselves by the level of their product and its quality. A deeper understanding of marketing wasn't necessary.

The growth of automation has created a new situation. Assembly lines began producing large numbers of identical products in a short amount of time. Supply could now exceed demand. Prices went down and the product itself became less important. Another factor was the development of factories in Asia, which could produce goods cheaply and in enormous quantities. As production quality grew, the products of different manufacturers became more similar to one another. The world population grew, as well as the general level of education. Many more people became qualified for skilled work. Information was readily available, and all kinds of production became possible. The result of technical progress and education is that products across manufacturers are of the same quality and cost the same. Quality is no longer an emphasized benefit today. We assume quality and consider it standard. There are even laws that contribute to this by enforcing a compulsory guarantee of the quality of goods.

In our current state of easily mass-produced supply, the question becomes *how can we generate steady demand*? How can we attract customers to our products and stores, when we ourselves know we're incapable of differentiating ourselves from our competitors by a large margin? As previously mentioned, this can't be resolved by the 4P mix. Marketing mindset had to move forward – from manufacturers and products to clients and solutions; from presentation to communication; from price to value; from product to solution.

Another important feature of developed economies is the abundance of everything. People don't worry so much about food, clothing, or transportation. Our society has evolved into a state where material goods are readily available and only a small group of people suffer. We are no longer in a position where we have to work all year to afford a new pair of shoes, or all day to pay for a decent meal.

The fulfillment of basic needs (food, housing, medical care, etc.) allows us to move up Maslow's hierarchy of needs and deal with more abstract topics. We turn our attention to experiences, self-development, emotions, self-realization, self-expression, and differentiation from others. Along with our new values come new demands on consumer goods. Clothing is no longer simply a means to cover our skin, so we don't get cold; it's now an expression of who we are. Some wear torn jeans, while others wear expensive, high-quality suits. Through our clothing, we express our emotions, our attitudes, and ourselves. The same is true for cars. At the beginning of the last century, cars were mainly a means of getting from one place to another. Today it's different. For many, their car is part of their lifestyle or an expression of luxury. People who care only about transportation will never understand the purchase of a Ferrari. We may think *"it's just a car"* but for Ferrari buyers, it certainly isn't.

When selling a Ferrari with a price tag in the hundreds of thousands, you're nowhere near the same market as economical car models. You need to build a whole other market with different purchasable goods. Emphasis on purchasable goods – this is the value that the client is buying. You may be selling a car, but the client is buying more than just a car. They are buying emotion, self-expression, social status, speed, freedom… or whatever else they imagine the brand says about them. Ferrari isn't in the same market as Ford, although they are both just cars from the product point of view.

New business demands can't be met by the 4P way of thinking. There is, however, a hitch. We mention how the 4P approach is intuitive to us; it promotes our egos and comfort zone. Unfortunately, it doesn't work in today's world. If we start a business using the 4P way of thinking, and not moving our attention to our customers, our new business is doomed to fail – even if we believe we have a completely new and groundbreaking product. Perhaps we have a head start with a completely new product, but it's only a matter of time before new competitors emerge in our market, with better access or lower prices.

Nokia is a particularly good example of a failure to innovate and apply a marketing mindset[12]. They were number one at the end of the last century. Half of the world's cell phones were Nokias. The company was innovative, delivering more features, smaller phones, better

---

[12] www.capitalandconflict.com/market-updates/money-morning-share-tips-nokia-10601/

sound quality, cameras, and more memory. In short, it was doing well for itself. Then something happened. Innovations in classic phones began to slow down while smartphones took off. In a short time, consumer requirements changed, along with purchasing behaviors and priorities.

Even a basic smartphone was already capable of much more than the traditional cell phone. New features, applications, and games were made available in droves. Advertisements focused on technical parameters attracted little interest as only a few people understood them. Add to this the fact that Chinese and Korean manufacturers, such as Lenovo or Samsung, managed to innovate fast and produce almost identical products at a lower price point. Their decision to combine their products with Android proved to be a good one. Nokia started to feel the consequences of being overly conservative and slow to change. Technology and the desires of clients were changing faster than the large corporation could keep up with.

This development resulted in the collapse and sale of Microsoft. The famous brand with its large market share declined steadily over a few years. It was the price of ignoring the changes in society and technology in an effort to stick to their old ways[13]. This clearly shows the evolution of the consumer economy. Those who do not adapt, do not survive. It makes no difference how successful a company was in the past.

---

[13] www.wired.com/2012/04/5-reasons-why-nokia-lost-its-handset-sales-lead-and-got-downgraded-to-junk/

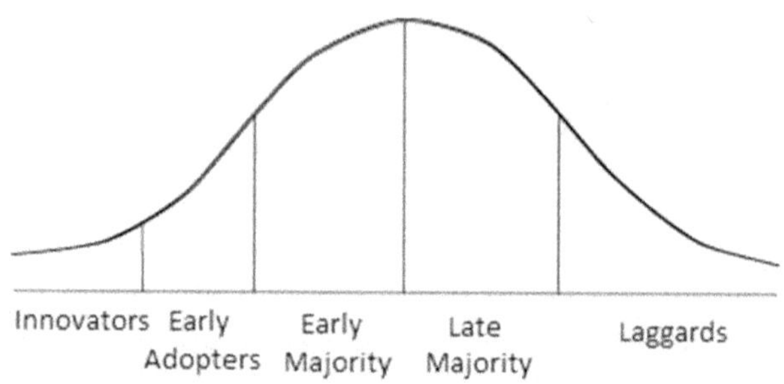

Diffusion of Innovations

Before describing the various stages of purchasing, we will learn about a theory called *"Diffusion of Innovation"*. The concept and theory were described in a book by Everett Rogers[14].

The theory of diffusion of innovation was initially introduced in the nineteenth century but described in more detail in the 1960s. Many of its elements are used in marketing theory to this day. The principle of market distribution applies across several disciplines, although exact numbers and divisions may vary.

The basis of the *diffusion of innovation* theory is shown in the graph above. It's a division of potential clients into five groups according to a Gaussian curve. Each group approaches innovative prod-

---

[14] Rogers M. Everett (1962). *Diffusion of Innovations*.

ucts differently. Knowledge of this theory and descriptions of individual groups will allow us to better target marketing campaigns. In other sections, we describe the stages of the purchasing process, which will differ according to the target market group based on the diffusion of innovation theory.

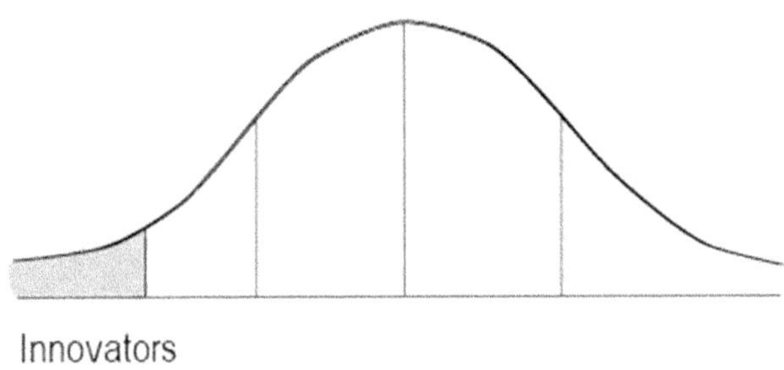

The Innovators

The first group is the innovators. This consists of around 2.5% of potential clients. This group is characterized by their openness to new ideas. When something new comes out, they want it. Innovators are often technologically oriented, and this effect is greatest when it comes to new electronic products. These customers immediately buy the latest phones, game consoles, computers, and appliances. They are excited by the novelty to such a degree that it hardly matters if they even need the product. Products quickly acquire the status of *outdated* for them and they are easily seduced by the latest model of something.

Innovators are an essential group for technology companies aiming to revolutionize the industry. A good example of this is Apple. Their iTunes revolutionized music distribution. In the beginning, it was the innovators who didn't hesitate to try it out and spread the news of their experience.

It's not a problem for innovators to try products that ultimately fail. They get emotional fulfillment from being among the first to try something.

If your business is innovative, the appropriate marketing platform might be crowdfunding. Innovators go here to look for interesting new products. When they like the idea, they support it financially. This also allows you to verify the marketability of your idea.

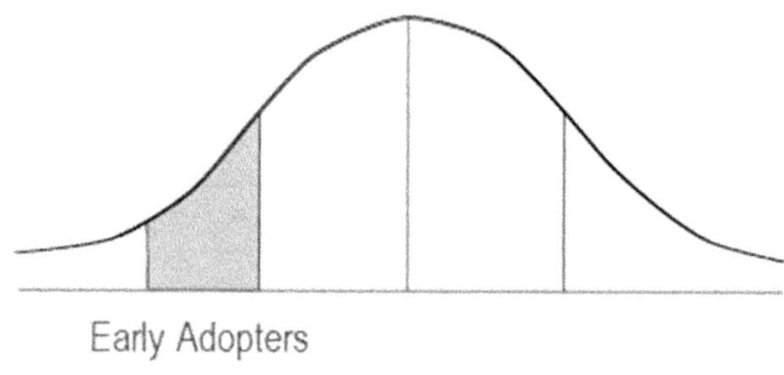

The Early Adopters

Early adopters form a much larger group than the innovators. They represent roughly 14% of the total market. Early adopters are curious and attracted by innovation. Unlike innovators, they think more carefully about their purchasing decisions. It's typical for members of this group to think through whether the novelty makes sense and if they need it. If they see potential in the product, they don't hesitate to invest in it.

As customers, early adopters are great because they appreciate new products and technological advances. They're willing to invest in a vision and don't require extensive demonstration of a product's functionality in order to try it out. They are prepared for small problems and are willing to participate in further improvement. For an innovative company, this group of clients is significant both commercially and as providers of useful information for how they can improve their product.

Early adopters are people who think ahead and want to improve themselves and their business. They are therefore open to new technologies, even when they come with a higher price or some uncertainties. They know that innovation is essential to competition.

To reach this group, we can present our early success within the innovator group. Innovators tend to be individuals or smaller companies than early adopters, but this isn't a problem. Early adopters tend to have insight and intellect at a level that enables them to recognize the potential of new technology.

In marketing, we make use of innovation and potential. This group responds to products that are not already modern and mainstream. They are delighted to discover something new and exploit its potential before others.

The Early Majority and the Late Majority

As innovations become more widespread, most people are now willing to join in. First, those who are open to innovations, and later, all those who are persuaded by the experiences of others. The early and late majorities account for approximately 34% of the market. To-gether, it's a group comprising 68% of potential customers.

The early majority will pay for new innovations only once the benefits are clearly demonstrated by the early adopter group. Its representatives had the opportunity to look at and touch the product and read the reviews of others' experiences.

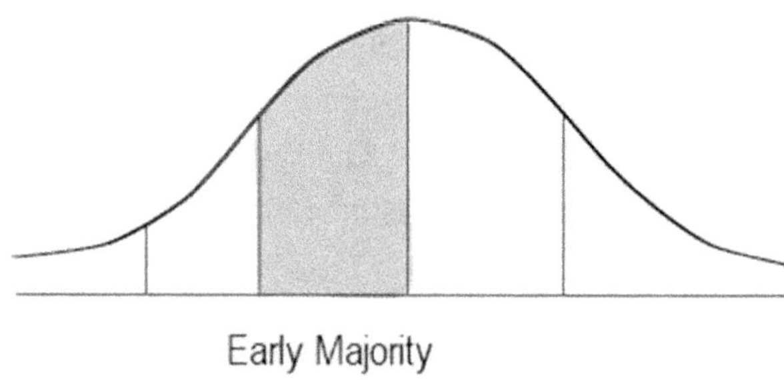

Early Majority

What is important for this group is stability and a sense of money well-invested. For them, the price is an important element in decision making. If an innovative product is too expensive, they will find satisfaction in an older model or pre-existing solution.

As the early majority becomes an overwhelming percentage of the clientele, they will exert pressure to lower the price. Increased demand lowers the price even further. This creates the right environment for the late majority to join in. These groups make up a third of all customers. The price was a major obstacle and they weren't as willing to invest in something based on novelty alone. When we want to target this group in marketing, we should adapt our campaign strategy accordingly.

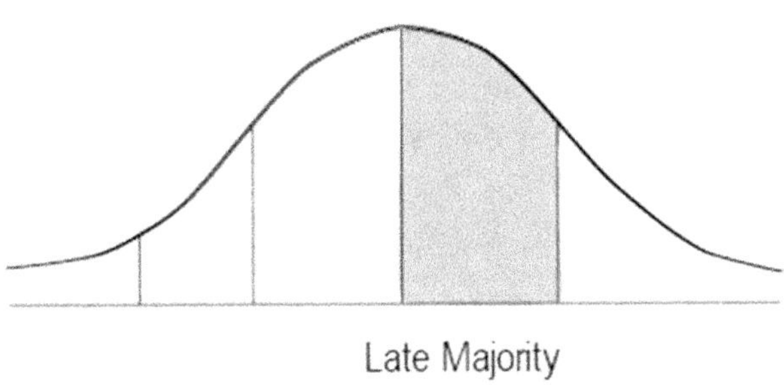

The characteristic trait of the late majority is submission to social pressure. You may remember the advent of mobile phones. Innovators were excited to be able to make phone calls without wall cords in the 1990s. Then the market widened to include all those who appreciated the benefits of their work. Communication became fast and easy. Among the late majority were people who didn't need a phone, and perhaps didn't even have a landline for a long time. This group only bought their mobile phones at the time when everyone else around them already had one. Mobile phone ownership became the standard and was expected of everyone. In the 90s, owning a cellphone was a rarity. Today, not owning one is a rarity.

The difference between the early and late majority is their willingness to spend money on novelty. For a given product, members of the early majority are willing to spend money sooner and in greater quantities. They want to invest in high-quality products. The late majority will exert the greatest pressure on the price point. Its representatives will seek out or require discounts and their decisions will be guided by incentives. Another factor will be social pressure. As the late majority isn't as technologically proficient, it can be difficult for them to assess the value of technological innovations. For example, this group will not respond to marketing campaigns that emphasize the speed of a mobile processor because they don't understand the technical language.

There is quite a big difference between the innovators and the late majority; in no case will the same marketing campaign work for both groups. Innovators are not seeking social approval. They want novelty, they want to be the first. Once something becomes mainstream, they have already lost interest.

Conversely, the late majority doesn't want to be first. Its members are skeptical and uninterested in trying out untested products. If the product hasn't already been seen in action, and its ease of use is still uncertain, then it's not worth the risk. The late majority places their trust in the opinions of their wider social group. If others don't have it, why should I? If others don't have it, it can't be all that useful.

You can see that each of the described groups will react differently, at different times, and to different information. To have good marketing, we must be clear on which group we are targeting and how we should go about communicating with them.

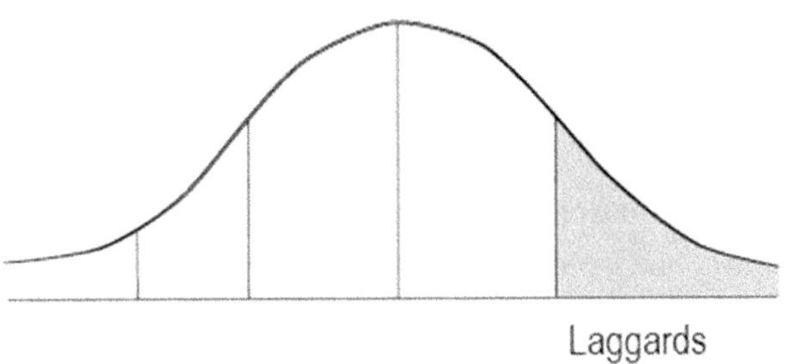

The Laggards

The laggards account for about 16% of the market. Members of this group can be further divvied up by how conservative they are. Laggards are characterized by great reluctance to buy or use new products and methods. When things have been done one way for 20 years, they see no reason to change course. This approach may be familiar in our grandparents. If you can beat eggs successfully by hand, there is no reason to go out and buy a mixer. Bread baked just fine in the regular oven, no need to spend extra on a dutch oven.

Marketing to the laggards isn't easy and they aren't particularly reactive. When attempting to bring in conservative customers, emphasis must be placed on how easy it is to transition to the new solution. These customers want to be sure that they will be able to handle the new method. Price is extremely important to this group, so there must be potential for discounts, non-binding trials, and easy returns.

Summary of *Diffusion of Innovations* And Examples

Understanding the different segments of the market will help build a better market strategy. In each field, the degree of innovation varies, along with the creativity of individual companies. Innovations made in the technology sector will be different from those in running shoes, or food service. It's impossible to give one set of instructions to all sectors. The theoretical model will help us keep in mind the more general categories into which we will substitute the target market variables. Brainstorming and external consultations are extremely important and beneficial at this stage.

Understanding how customers perceive innovation along with a working knowledge of marketing mixes will make sales much easier. We can avoid the situation of peddling something we have a low potential of selling to a customer who is unappreciative of the product's value. Here's a classic example...

Grandma and the smartphone dealer

Salesperson: Check it out, this smartphone is incredible. 16GB RAM, 12-megapixel camera, internet, calendar, storage for hundreds of contacts, and thousands of apps on Android!

Grandmother: But where are the buttons?

Salesperson: The smartphone has a touch screen. You don't need buttons. Look, this has an 8" screen.

Grandmother: A touch...what??

Salesperson: You tap directly on the screen. There is no need for buttons.

Grandmother: Jeez, I might accidentally break it. What about those 16 giga-somethings; what does that mean? I can only call to 16 other phone numbers?

Salesperson: No, no. That's the amount of memory. You can save whatever you want directly on your phone.

Grandmother: I don't want to save things to my phone, I want buttons and calling. And big numbers so I can read them. How much does a phone like that cost?

Salesperson: This is the latest model; it's only $700.

Grandmother: Come on, you're crazy. That much? I only need to know how to make a phone call.

Salesperson: Of course, it can do phone calls. Take a look...

Grandmother: But you didn't tell me it could make phone calls! You tell me about Giga-whatevers, I don't even know what that means. Can I call my daughter?

Salesperson: Of course, you can even store her number into the contacts.

Grandmother: I don't need to store anything; I have her number written down here in my little notebook…

This is the way sales conversations can look with a completely non-prospective customer. Sometimes you'll be successful in selling something, but margins of success will remain slim. Moreover, if we continue to do business with the 4P model, we won't even be thinking about what Grandma wants. We're still going to want to sell whatever we have in our hands. It seems that a more effective approach is just a matter of common sense – listen more and find solutions for our customers. Unfortunately, experience shows that entrepreneurs like to repeat the same known mistakes. In the chapter, Predictably Irrational, I will describe the phenomenon of the non-critical perception of our products.

How the market of air travel has evolved

Innovation doesn't always mean new technology. Companies must adjust to their customers' shopping behaviors and habits. This puts companies in the position of trying to predict future behaviors and allocate resources to their predictions. Air travel is an excellent example.

For many years, Boeing had the largest airliner in the world. Airbus anticipated that the demand for large aircraft would grow and invested hundreds of millions of dollars into developing a newer, bigger model. This is how the stunning A380 aircraft was created.

Airbus assumed that there would be several large airports around the world – hubs, such as London or Dubai – to which passengers would travel on larger planes, and then fly to smaller airports closer to their final destinations on smaller planes. As the air travel industry developed and low-cost airlines emerged, passengers began to take flights to multiple destinations at many times throughout the day. Passengers no longer had the patience to wait for a big aircraft to fill up. Some passengers need to depart at 6 am, some at 8, and some at 10. These behaviors were easily met by airlines with smaller aircraft. Large aircraft, such as the A380 began to struggle with occupancy and thus production and profits.

Currently, the A380 is in decline and the only Dubai-based Emirates is buying these planes new. The location in Dubai plays a role, but even for Emirates, occupancy can be a problem. It seems the time for the giant aircraft may have passed.

The example with large planes and air travel habits demonstrates how large companies have to bet their investments on how they expect the market to develop. If their predictions are incorrect, they will lose money. In today's rapidly developing society, it helps to have an overview of possible development pathways. Sometimes, companies get lucky or make an accidentally advantageous investment. Entrepreneurship relies a bit on luck, but remember, *luck favors the prepared!*

Social development means companies must change their approach to recruiting new employees

Many countries currently have record low unemployment levels. The long-term levels hover as low as 1%. For employers, this creates a situation most companies are not used to – labor shortage. Companies must use active marketing to even attract talent to their workforce. Vague job advertisements may not elicit any responses. Potential employees are not only interested in salaries, but in the company itself, working conditions, team culture, client base, and management style. Companies face pressure to make job offers attractive. Additionally, if companies don't respond quickly to interested individuals, require multiple interviews, or are not polite and friendly in interactions, candidates will quickly look elsewhere for employment offers.

Companies that manage their recruits well also tend to manage their employees well. It's precisely these types of companies that don't face the problems of a few applicants and high turnover rates.

It may seem that discussing recruitment in a chapter about innovation is unusual, but innovation on the labor market ties into business success. New ways of thinking spread between companies. Some adapt quickly and gain a strong market advantage, while others stagnate because they can't attract enough reliable people to carry out the volume of orders necessary to grow.

Phases of Purchasing Process

Several phases occur in the process of a customer making a purchase. These phases must be considered for a successful sale. Individual phases may be sped-up but not skipped over, otherwise, the salesperson will present a potential client with information and opportunities they aren't yet engaged in or interested in. When this happens, the client may lose enthusiasm, feel coerced, or simply decide to shop around for other options.

In this chapter, I will describe the purchasing stages, and highlight what kind of information is relevant for customers at each stage. The process may differ slightly in different fields, but the basic structure remains the same. Make your own description of each phase based on your personal business endeavor. Just thinking about your client's situation will help you to orient yourself in these processes, and thus market and sell your product more effectively.

#1 The Client Realizes There Is An Issue To Address

People tend to put off solving their everyday problems. Sometimes we know we need to make a change long before we attempt to do anything about it; whether we want to lose weight, quit smoking, start a business, improve our skills or whatever else. We know something needs to be done.

Occasionally, we're presented with a solution that makes us realize we can fix something we didn't even realize was broken (or simply less than ideal). There are plenty of things we aren't aware of that could make our lives more streamlined. For example, if you're uninterested in technology, you probably don't know or care that there are already autonomous lawn-mowing robots that can cut your grass for you. You know about gas and electric lawnmowers, but the idea of a robot probably never occurred to you. That is, until you see it in an ad, read about it in an article, or see one rolling around your neighbor's yard.

Imagine a person realizing that they need to solve a problem. It could be anything: they need to buy food, wash their car, build a house, learn to draw or update their professional training. At this moment, this person is a potential client for someone. What happens next? Let's take a look at the phases of purchasing, from a potential client first deciding to fix their situation, to finally making a purchase.

#2 Looking For Solutions

For many problems, consumers don't have to think twice about how to solve them. We want food, we go to the supermarket. We need gasoline, we go to the gas station. But there are professions and services we don't even know about yet. Groceries are a good example. A brick and mortar shop will come to mind first. Another option might be a food delivery service, which in recent times is making appearances in cities all over the world.

Finding new solutions requires additional time and research. We don't always have the energy or desire to do this. It's easier to simply make our decision based on some recommendations we heard or an article we read. Generally, the more expensive the purchase, the longer we spend considering options.

While looking for solutions, information, and option evaluation is particularly important for the client. For now, the price is not so important, as long as it isn't excessively high. The brand or company offering the solution also isn't particularly important for the customer, yet (except in some cases of extreme brand loyalty, such as with Apple Inc.). If our product isn't well-known on the market yet, we need to focus on this stage. We must tell our potential clients what our new product is and how it can help them. Focusing on price or brand is useless at this stage. The client isn't deciding to buy a new product, one they are not yet even sure they need, based on whether you're a *"young, dynamic company"*.

If you're selling a product with a clear purpose, then this phase will go by quickly. When the client knows they want shoes, they're prepared to entertain offers on shoes. They're probably not going to explore the possibilities of skin implants on their feet just so they can walk barefoot.

So far, this is general information to help orient your product or service in the market. The next phase of the purchase results in product type awareness.

#3 Brand Recognition

Marketing should work so that the client knows our brand and what solutions our company can offer them. A consumer's first impression of a brand is important, but prepare yourself for the fact that the prevailing feeling will be a lack of trust at first. It's the seller's job to earn confidence!

Different people behave differently at the brand recognition stage. This partially depends on where the group falls according to the *Diffusion of Innovation* model. Innovators react completely differently to certain stimuli than the Late Majority. Some are interested in web presence and graphics. Others look at a company's portfolio, products, prices, or media images. Innovators are attracted to new and unconventional solutions.

Many customers search the internet for reviews and feedback from other users. In the last decade, online reviews have become an extremely important part of making decisions in purchasing. Some statistics indicate that 84% of shoppers trust online reviews and make decisions according to them.

This brings up the question of how to deal with fake reviews and articles paid for directly by the seller. There has been a great deal of progress in this area in recent years. People still trust online reviews because they have adapted and learned to spot fake or poorly written reviews and filter them out. Online reviews are also dependent on the ability of the buyers to give informative feedback. Some websites ask their clients to answer specific questions about their experience. When you read a decidedly negative review written in a rough and offensive style, one can imagine that the customer might be the source of more problems than the actual product itself. Profanity about a company or product has no informative value. If there are only a few negative reviews, you shouldn't worry about their impact. At the same time, it's recommended you respond to negative reviews if you're in a position to set the record straight.

Reviews that are written factually, give concrete examples, and summarize the pros and cons are the most informationally valuable. Customers have learned what reviews are valuable, and most people try to write such reviews. Especially as names of verified clients appear on many sites, people are less likely to hide behind an anonymous profile.

Building brand awareness is important for company reputation and client interest. It's not the only decision-making factor, but it's an important one. Potential clients are examining other brands in direct and indirect competition. The question is, how to attract them enough that they give up on competing brands and do business with us?

This is a challenge for marketers since there is little time to present the story of the brand and all the value it brings. The more competition exists, the less time customers are willing to give individual companies. The situation is even more demanding for e-shops than brick-and-mortar ones. When you walk into a physical store, chances are you won't leave it immediately in a matter of seconds. On a website, people change their minds instantaneously–Close the tab and look for another site to click on. Statistics say that on average over 50% of people leave a page within 15 seconds. The impatience and split-second decision making of modern shoppers challenges marketers and their strategies.

A brand's *story* is most interesting to clients, although it's often overlooked. It's our human need to belong somewhere and not to feel alone. We are reluctant to make decisions that go against the crowd. Whenever we enter a store, whether in-person or online, we need to feel as quickly as possible that we belong there. Project the feeling that the environment suits the clients and they will find value there. This is the role of the story.

This differs greatly from the 4P model. Many companies try to compete based on 4P, but soon find that their only weapon is the price. Even this is limited by a certain minimum, below which having business no longer makes sense. Price competition is a dangerous game that doesn't work for long. Moreover, it's only the biggest player, who benefits from sheer volume, that can compete on this level. Large volume allows them to provide a much lower price than any small shop is capable of. For example, Amazon works with margins of only a few percent. Their total profit is given by huge turnovers. But if we open a new site or a new business, with a margin of around 6%, it makes no sense economically. What does this imply? Some sales strategies are doomed to fail even before they start. It's good to find these things out fast and think of a plan before spiraling into spending more and more money.

To succeed in a competitive environment, the best practice is to eliminate the competition as much as possible, until ideally, none remains. How to accomplish this? You won't find this in 4P. If we move from 4P to SIVA, we suddenly have limitless creative possibilities to attract customers, even if the product itself remains similar to the competition.

As I wrote earlier in this chapter on marketing mixes, when selling a car, it's luxury, speed, and freedom that the customer is buying. Thinking like this will cut down your competition drastically. If you sell watches, then you have hundreds of competitors, and each retailer has hundreds of seemingly identical models. What's with that? Well, you can create a super-luxury brand where the price of the watch doesn't matter – Reach the world's richest clients and sell them watches as an expression of style and luxury with price tags in the hundreds of thousands. Now you're no longer competing with the $200 watches. Meanwhile, a very different sector of the watch-buying market will react more favorably to the high-tech wonders of watches that come equipped with smartphone-like features, or extra durable watches for climbers that are shock-resistant, or special watches designed for deep-water diving.

Whatever section of the market you chose to sell to, using a marketing mindset will help you filter out a significant amount of competition. Once the competition is filtered, we can see our target clients clearly and communicate with them directly to better meet their needs. Having a filtered subset of the market isn't only easier to distribute information to, but the potential clients it reaches will be more interested in learning about our brand.

Products of different brands in one store

A complex marketing situation arises when shop owners sell different brands in one place: a shoe or cosmetics store, for example. These sellers can't use brand names to advertise their wares due to licensing and trademark laws.

It's necessary to devise a clear differentiation from the competition. For the products, we can offer more choices, lower prices, promotions, or favorable exchange policies. The options for products are quite limited and easy to copy.

To use the example of the shoe store, one solution can be to develop services and advice based around footwear in general. As an example, let's look at different brands of athletic shoes. Athletes want more than just a quality pair of shoes; they want a shoe that will fit their individual proportions and foot shape. A good athletic shoe store can offer on-site measuring. From there, they can recommend the most suitable shoe. In this way, a store can maintain high variety and provide added value over similar stores.

If you sell expensive electronics, you can offer payment in installments, free or reduced-price installation with purchase, insurance policies for mobile phones and cameras, and other services that make life easier for your customers.

Section Summary

In the phase of *Building Brand Awareness*, the client is interested in whether they can identify with our company. They want to know if they can buy something of reasonable value, yet the value can be somewhat abstract. If were to continue building a relationship with our clients, we need to show that we share the same attitudes and understand their needs.

In this stage, neither the product nor the price is very important because the client isn't yet ready to compare it. At this stage, customers usually don't fully comprehend the total amount of value offered, meaning the price will always seem high.

The most important take-away is that there is no time to waste making a good impression. In the real world, you have a matter of minutes to impress customers: online, just a few seconds.

#4 Building Intrigue Through Stories And Emotions

The goal here is to keep the attention of potential clients. We want them interested in our brand and in new products as they become available. In this stage, the benefit to the client is still more important than the product itself. We aren't selling face cream – we are selling a beautiful complexion. We don't provide accounting services –we provide reliability and peace-of-mind. Our product isn't an expensive watch - our product is the feeling of luxury.

The clients are not seeking a specific product, they are looking to improve their life. At this stage, we don't have the loyalty that guarantees sales from our company. Deciding to buy something is an emotional decision that is later rationalized. The less rational the person, the less they are interested in straight facts, and the more they seek emotional stimuli.

Nothing arouses the emotions like a good story. A good story consists of experience, real-life situations, and original solutions to various challenges. Typical motifs are as follows: conquering obstacles, gaining motivation, inspiring others, overcoming difficult life situations, helping the world, or caring for people, nature, or animals. We want to achieve feelings of joy, determination, belonging, hope, appreciation, admiration, pride, and satisfaction. Each person is looking for patterns which they would like to emulate, whether in sports, business, or their profession. If we can provide such a pattern, it's easy to find people that we will inspire and who can identify with our story. Once they can identify with our brand, they will follow our activity and give preference to our products and services.

Example. Compare two approaches to selling the same product – a fitness/weight loss program. First approach: the course is prepared by a personal trainer but sold by an unspecialized salesperson – someone out of shape, uninformed about nutrition, and generally uninterested in the goal of the course. The seller is completely disconnected from the product, aside from the obvious desire to make some fast money.

Second approach: a similar course is offered by a trainer who is actively engaged in fitness activities, runs daily, has an exemplary figure, and shares their healthy recipes on their social media. They have put the course together and are the primary instructor.

Which seller would you choose? Where can you follow the story? A person who takes any old product and tries to sell it has very limited potential. When the product is seen as nothing more than a commodity, it's difficult to impress buyers.

In the second case, the trainer lived the story and the goal of what they want to share with others. The product contains their heart, soul, and personality. It's not just a collection of workouts and dietary advice. It's a connection to the author, and a healthier, more fulfilling lifestyle.

What is the main difference between a freelancer and a big firm at this stage of sales? A freelancer may share their personal story or the successes their past clients achieved with their help.

Big companies have other options they can use. First and foremost, it's the personal story of the founder and their vision for the business they created. The second strong motive is corporate culture, client care, innovativeness, environmental interests, and the like. To use this, companies can demonstrate the satisfaction of their clients and how their lives have improved.

Example. One smaller coffee company is based on fair trade – i.e. promoting fair financing for African farmers. On their website, they have different types of coffee available, but they also actively present their activities in the communities where they cultivate their product. The company spends time in the community, funds education for the people there, and takes care of ecological cultivation practices. They managed to connect coffee, as a product, with people and their destinies. When buying coffee from this company, you have the feeling that your purchase is having a positive economic impact thousands of miles away. From just selling coffee, this company has managed to create an admirable story with a strong human dimension.

At the end of this section, we will introduce another type of sales situation, where the phases of #4 and #5 merge and depend more on the product than the seller. Examples include computer and mobile games. Games in which the users can create a story on their own – the creator doesn't need to be well known. The aim of the games is primarily relaxation, escaping from reality into diverse environments. Simulation, shooter, strategy games, or RPGs: Each type of game creates a different environment and supports different experiences.

Example. The famous Czech game Mafia has won many awards for its elaborate story. The game brings you into the 1930s in the role of a mafia gangster. Many people are fascinated by organized crime and stories about the Mafia in the United States. Mafia the game makes people part of that story, which makes it both attractive to players and a very successful business venture. The graphics and a great variety of gameplay situations are a big plus for the quality of the game, but the story was truly a crucial factor in its success.

Business and marketing between companies – B2B[15]

In some fields, it may appear that emotions play no role whatsoever. For example, large technological orders, production lines, machines, and so on. In industrial fields, the situation is complex, and the marketing approach differs considerably from the presentation of a small businessman who sells his accounting services. What is the basis of

---

[15] B2B stands for Business to Business – i.e. selling to other companies

large-scale business transactions? In one word, **trust**. The technology itself doesn't have to build any emotions; all that matters is that it functions reliably. But remember, there is always a person in charge of making purchasing decisions. We must earn their trust. This trust is built on a long-term basis and is strengthened through consistent availability, sustained interest, proven expertise, and a track record of jobs well done.

Buyers need to know that the solution we provide will work reliably and that we will be responsible for taking care of any problems. These characteristics are judged not only on the personality of the salesperson, but also on the history of the company, fulfilled orders, personal references, and of course, company culture and the human factor. To focus only on the product when selling is to miss out on an important advantage in business. Our competition is suggesting similar solutions. We don't want to find ourselves in a situation where changing the quantity justifies the value. This unpleasant situation may culminate in economic inefficiency or direct losses.

The solution to this is to connect the people in our company with the product. Highlight the company's culture, expertise, references, and human approach – assets people care about. If you find yourself competing for a business opportunity, it may be advantageous to emphasize past accounts of workers solving problems for clients. It's important to present your company as being reliable and having a positive work attitude.

Devising a strategy to attract clients to our brand requires a lot of creative work and especially communication with the target market. The use of external assistance in the form of consultations is always beneficial.

Example: I tagged along with some business partners from a medium-sized IT company at a meeting with a large corporation. The IT company had recently been selected to do some work for the large corporation, and the woman in charge of the collaboration specifically praised the presentation the IT company had prepared for the selection process. She mentioned that the presentation made it clear that they were detail-oriented, and it was an important factor in their decision to collaborate with this company.

This anecdote demonstrates how applying for a large IT contract turns into an evaluation of both the presentation and the presenters. It's not so much the complex technology, but the diligence, perceived expertise, pleasant demeanors, and ability to present ideas that become decisive factors. These are important even in the case of technologically driven products and services. A humanistic approach makes a big difference.

#5 The Customer Is Interested In The Details of The Product

The client is now so impressed, they're willing to devote some time to learn more. They're interested to know how we're different from other brands. We present mainly originality and a personal approach. The products themselves depend on the level of difference from the competition. The customer is interested in our approach and whether they will work well with us. In this phase, we're now building trust and it's very important not to lose it, as getting it back can be costly and time-consuming.

In the previous chapter, we indicated that the transition from phase #4 to #5 is different in various fields. Much depends on whether you're a standalone entrepreneur, a small business, or a large company supplying extensive solutions. This book focuses on entrepreneurs, and small to medium-sized businesses, where personalities and stories play a larger role. Therefore, the following examples are targeted to a small business environment.

At this phase, we distinguish between:

♦ The customer who already uses products from our competition: they know what they're looking for in a product. This type of customer is more informed; the goal of marketing is primarily to present the difference in our company's quality and approach. They know what the other options are. Complications with winning over this type of customer arise if they're conservative or unwilling to change their habits. In particular, clients that are already satisfied with their current solution are reluctant to spend money on something new. For them, even a lower price or a discount isn't going to change their mind.

♦ The customer who doesn't yet use any similar products. This customer doesn't have a lot of knowledge about the benefits of the product offered. It's best to inform them of the most important information and practical advantages to *your* solution over the competition. For this client, price isn't a driving factor because they have nothing to compare it to yet. They require time and information. Coercion, forced-action, loyalty programs, and discounts will not work on this customer.

#6 The Client Is Interested In Our Product

The time has come to explain to the client, why they should work with you and not your competition. Now it's important to show off your customer support, positive reviews, business ratings, and any other data that highlights how your company stacks up to the competition. At this point, price begins to play an important role but still isn't essential (unless our explicit business model is the lowest price possible). We have traveled a long way up to the pre-purchase stage and now we have a potential customer. The task of the salesperson is to simplify the decision. Discounts and incentives may work to reduce the reluctance to hand over money. Less expensive product variants may help – trial versions, smaller packages, etc. Here the goal is to sell the client anything, even if we don't make a large profit. We want to present our solution and the experience of working with our company, and gradually build brand loyalty.

#7 The Client Made A Purchase

An important goal has now been fulfilled! Congratulations, but the process doesn't end here. What you want is for your clients to be so satisfied that they recommend your business to their friends and leave positive reviews of your goods or services online. You can now present your client with incentives for purchasing with you again and offer benefits through loyalty programs.

Let's distinguish between 3 typical situations

- **The enthusiastic client.** This is the ideal state. Your client is satisfied with your product. Your subsequent task becomes getting them to purchase from your company again in the future. Because they are already satisfied, the price isn't an important factor. To simplify comparisons, you can develop a few variants of your product for purchase. For example, a set of products at a bargain price, 2 + 1 free, a lower price for bulk purchases, etc. You want to maintain continuous communication with your enthusiastic client, especially as they're increasingly valuable in expanding brand awareness. It's important to maintain the relationship and personal touch that your client appreciates – whether through more purchases or on social media. Remember, the client is building a relationship with people, not just the brand.

- **The dissatisfied client**. This is a more complex situation that requires patience and tact. The client may not always be right and may even be fundamentally wrong. In all cases, however, you must maintain your professionalism and come up with some solutions for consideration. Angry clients are very motivated to slander businesses on social networks and leave exaggeratedly negative reviews, which then discourage undecided buyers. Sometimes it's better to accommodate the client, even when they're not right, to avoid conflict. Every situation is unique and requires a careful approach. We will continue this discussion in the chapter on marketing processes.

- ♦ **The "okay" client**. This situation can be difficult to grasp. The client isn't dissatisfied, but the "wow" effect is missing. They won't complain on social media, but also probably won't leave positive feedback. When addressed directly, this client will tell us that their purchase with us was "okay". This kind of feedback has no value whatsoever to the seller.

This last class of customers highlights room for improvement. There is only a short period to win them over for a second purchase. If you don't follow up with them, they'll likely turn to other similar products and services.

A company can still have a productive relationship with this type of customer, but only if it's willing to address the customers' reservations. Various tools in online marketing can help: Targeted advertising, remarketing, direct reach, or personal discounts via email. With email marketing, for example, we may only have one chance before our target client unsubscribes from further newsletters.

Summary of The Purchasing Process And Examples

Understanding the purchasing process from our clients' point of view can help you to better adapt to the various phases purchases are made from. In this way, you can provide all potential clients with the right information at the moment when they will react most favorably to it.

So far, I have emphasized how a story, originality, trust, and the human element are the factors that can make or break a sale. For a product, the price isn't as important as the value the buyer perceives the product to have, and this can be quite abstract. It is, therefore, necessary to present products with a background of *abstract value* that is meaningful to the client.

Emotion plays a major role in all stages. A self-made entrepreneur can use the originality of their own life story to inspire interest and loyalty in clients. This may complement the stories of satisfied clients who used the product to achieve a specific goal. Larger companies can leverage their expertise, corporate culture, innovative successes, personal approach, and emphasize the personality of their founder. Corporate narratives can also be drawn from the completion of major projects.

Making a sale may mark the end of the purchasing cycle, but the work doesn't end there. We want clients not only to come back but also to recommend our services and products to those around them. **The best marketing is the one that someone else does for us, and for free!** We will only achieve this if our clients are extremely satisfied and excited about collaborating with us again.

Examples of Marketing Communication

Marking communication is more than just talking. It's all the ways information gets to our potential clients. We can consider a blackboard standing outside a bar to be marketing, for example. Once you start paying attention to what you see on billboards, posters, flyers, and ad spots, you can begin to evaluate how you perceive these ads and use it as a springboard in your marketing mindset.

A board outside a bar: Outdoor seating, free Wi-Fi.

Suppose this is a pub that we're not familiar with. What do you think about their communication? According to the previous section on the phases of the purchasing process, we're at phase 4. We are wondering if the pub is worth stepping into. Does the blackboard address this? It is luring us in? Well, we can't say if we care about the outdoor seating because we aren't yet sure we want to stop here. Wi-Fi might have been a service ten years ago, but now it's taken as standard in almost all places. Moreover, we go to a pub for beer and food, rather than for Wi-Fi. This blackboard has effectively wasted its potential to attract new customers.

Restaurant Board: Lunch special $5

Price highlighting is a common element in marketing communications. But how is such a message received? Is the potential customer saying, *"Hooray, lunch for $5!"*, or are they thinking, *"Hmmm, that price seems low, I can't be any good."* If a low price is not the only strategy you have, then presenting only low prices outside your restaurant isn't a good idea. As previously mentioned, the price isn't relevant to the customer yet because the customer isn't sure if they're even interested in your product. A high price is discouraging because it can immediately turn off customers. A low price can be equally dangerous as customers may associate it with low quality. The take-home message here is that presentation of product prices at the beginning of the sales process will do more harm than good. And yet, we see prices in a vast majority of advertisements.

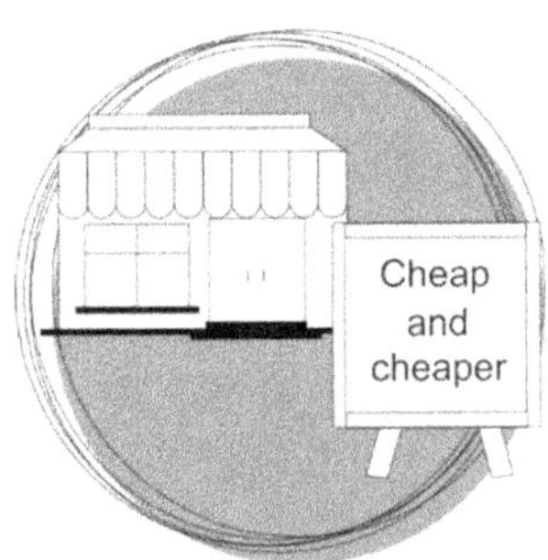

Tip: Prices should not be displayed outside. The customer is not interested until they have decided to go inside. Announcing the prices will not draw more people in; it will only deter them or have no effect. In any case, it's a waste of marketing space, and, since the boards that stand in front of buildings in larger cities must be paid for, it's also a waste of money.

Tip: After reading the phases of purchasing chapter, you'll probably be able to come up with considerably better marketing messages. The goal is to arouse interest and emotion. The board is tasked with stopping passersby and making them think about visiting your business.

Example: Delicious goulash, served with freshly baked bread; Fragrant homemade apple pie; French-style crepes with fresh fruit; Taste the exotic with a cup of our Columbian coffee; Experience the great atmosphere of a classic American pub.

There are endless ways to impress passersby. Use external marketing space to appeal to customers' senses and awaken their curiosity. Remember there is a difference between *what a shop sells* and *what a customer buys*. You may sell steaks, but the customer is buying a gastronomic experience.

Advertising poster: Vacuum cleaner for $250.

Many public places are filled with small advertising posters of this type. To best take advantage of the limited space, it's necessary to think about the situation of the passengers who will see the poster. A metro ride lasts only a few minutes and there isn't much to do. Mobile internet doesn't work very well, and when there are a lot of people, even reading a book can be very uncomfortable. Not wanting to seem like they are staring, people tend to avoid direct eye contact with other passengers. This creates an environment for looking at ads. They don't disturb us; they're not invasive, and we have time to read the message. The chances of remembering text are much greater than, for example, from billboards on the highway.

For us marketers, all the advantages are on our side. And yet a highlighted price almost always appears on the posters. You have already learned that this is simply bad practice. This goes double for products like electronics and appliances, which people don't just buy based on how cheap they are. Maybe we buy a vacuum cleaner because we want a cleaner apartment, office, or car. What we expect in a device is that it handles well, has decent power, and can easily be cleaned. For potential clients, the price is uninteresting because there is nothing to compare it to and the price is not a major deciding factor when it comes to electronics. When did it happen to you that you enthusiastically called out to your partner: "H*ey, Honey, can you believe it? There is a vacuum cleaner for only $250. We have to buy it right now!*"? I would guess it hasn't – and probably never will happen.

The example clearly illustrates how hard it is to create advertising material according to the 4P model. If we don't address our clients' needs, all our advertising material will be boring and blur into every other uninteresting ad they encounter.

What can we emphasize about electronics? Firstly, the purchasing of electronics usually involves time to make comparisons and assess technical parameters. These things don't fit well on small posters. If a metro poster is the way we want to go about advertising, we must focus on the benefit to the client and awaken their curiosity about our product. The poster should generate interest in the product, and leave the client thinking that they should look for more information about it later.

Example: Do you know that x% of vacuum cleaners won't get rid of mites in your carpet? We present a solution to this with model XYZ! It comes with an extended warranty and interest-free payment in installments.

A similar message will impress and make onlookers think. If they can remember the brand name, there's a good chance they'll be looking for more information. Some will then end up buying a new vacuum cleaner. Not because of the price! But because of the benefit, they're receiving – a cleaner home.

How A Salesman Talked Us Out of Buying A Stroller. A Story.

As a marketer, I always pay close attention to the different tactics salespeople try on me. I appreciate it when the salesperson tries to help me find a solution, rather than coercing me into a sale. Occasionally, it happens that either a salesperson or someone in marketing does such a poor job that they ruin a potential sale or even talk the customer out of buying the product.

For our newborn son, my wife and I were searching for a stroller from a well-known premium brand. We found a store that carried this brand. The young salesman was very helpful; he showed us everything and explained how the stroller worked. He even told us that he had the same stroller at home and was highly satisfied. It would be his first choice. We left with a good feeling. The salesman told us that an order takes about 3 months to fulfill.

We had come to the store well in advance of our son's birth intending to order a stroller and pay a deposit. We met another salesman, not as friendly as the previous one, but he showed us the stroller and confirmed it would be a good choice. We asked about ordering it and he told us it was complicated, and the order would take a long time to be fulfilled. (Remember that when selling, the goal is to solve issues for the client and offer solutions. This salesman was producing new problems.) We told him that his colleague had already let us know that an order would take 3 months and we had come to the store with this timeline in mind. Then my wife said, *"Perhaps it'll be faster to order one online"*. This should cause a warning to go off in every good salesperson's mind that they are about to lose a customer if they're already

131

considering buying online. Our salesman caught this but astonishingly confirmed: "*Yes, it would be faster on the Internet*". The situation became absurd. We had come to the store to put a deposit down on a stroller and the salesman talked us out of the sale.

When we got home, out of a certain loyalty to the store, we pulled up their website and started configuring the stroller we wanted for our son. Soon the website encountered technical difficulties and we were unable to get the version of the stroller we wanted.

We went instead to the website of the seller who specialized in this particular brand of stroller. The site worked great and they even called us personally to explain delivery conditions, recommend suitable accessories, and offered us the opportunity to view other products in their Prague location. Their approach was perfect. We ordered the stroller and in three months, it came.

The first salesman did great work; he helped us decide on a premium stroller – the most expensive in the store. In the end, another salesman spoiled the sale with his poor approach and convinced us not to buy through the store. The disaster was finalized by a non-functional website. In the end, the company didn't get our order and very likely, the orders of others like us.

Remember that there is more to marketing than advertising. It's the whole process, and it doesn't end even at the point of sale. Good marketing includes sales followed by great service and appropriate recommendations of other products –upsell. We ended up buying several more accessories for our new stroller from the specialized retailer.

The See – Think – Do – Care Model

The STDC model, or framework as it's sometimes called, is a system that allows us to divide marketing into parts and divide clients into segments. This is a tool, similar to the marketing mixes, that allows you to divide and conquer your target audience using targeted marketing campaigns. The idea is to work with individual sections of the target audience separately, using various marketing techniques.

Example. Consider a job portal in a large company and think about what type of visitors come and what part of the STDC model they belong to.

A visitor may come to the website for the first time after having clicked on an advertisement or memorizing a billboard or web address. This visitor is just getting acquainted with the company or brand, so we shouldn't expect any action from them yet. Before we gain the visitor's trust, we can't force any registration forms, discounts, or purchases on them, or they will leave our site to avoid the pressure.

People who are coming to a website for the first time are looking for information about the solution you are providing, and how it will add value to their lives. In the SIVA marketing mix, these are S – *"solution"* and V – *"value"*. Visitors may not be interested in purchasing right away.

The *"See"* phase doesn't necessarily take place on the website – it can be on a forum, blog, social media network, or consumer comparison report, or even offline at a trade show, conference, or workshop.

The goal of the *"See"* phase is to present solutions, meaning it's too early to talk price, discounts, or loyalty programs without seeming coercive. Focus on advertising, building brand awareness and recognition. Draw potential clients in to look at the company website, social media profile, or storefront.

Think. The *"Think"* phase is characterized by the visitor's interest in the website and learning more about the product or service. The potential customer may want to ask about details over live chat, email, phone, or social media. The sales teams should be able to reliably answer common questions and know enough about the competition to present the strengths of the product they represent.

In the example of a job portal, the visitor spends time browsing multiple pages. If the visitor is currently looking for a job, they can register and get more information.

When a customer decides to purchase something, they need to know it will resolve a problem. This is clear for products like clothes and food. More complex goods and services may need additional explanation. For example, a new online meeting hosting platform, a warehouse management application, or an accounting service. Articles, blog posts, videos, and case studies will all help get the message to the prospective buyer.

Do. The action in the *"Do"* phase may be different, depending on the context. For online sellers, it's a purchase, or for larger services, it will be contacting the dealer for a quote. For subscription-based services, the *"Do"* phase will be setting up an account or downloading an application. For restaurants and storefronts, it will be customers coming in and spending money.

Bringing a visitor from the *"Think"* phase to the *"Do"* phase may require getting them to return to your site more than once. This is typically accomplished by reminding the visitor, either through marketing campaigns, social media ads, or personal contact information.

Care. The *"Care"* phase is often overlooked. If you remember from the chapter on marketing mixes and the purchasing process, we mentioned how it's cheaper and more efficient to make additional sales to existing customers than it is to seek out and sell to new customers. That's why it's very important to pay attention to the *"Care"* phase. Be aware of your clients after they make their purchase. What did they do with the product, how have they reviewed it, would they recommend it to others? Are they satisfied? Have unsatisfied customers had their grievances addressed? What do customers like the most and can we use that information to make the product even better in the future? These are all good questions to follow up on. Having the answers is a valuable resource to build up and further develop the brand. If the *"Care"* phase is ignored, it will be necessary to find and chase new clients at a higher cost.

In the example of the job portal, we should consider the people who successfully found a job through our service. Do we have any way of keeping in touch with them? Will they come back in 2 or 3 years if they want to look for a new job? Will they recommend our portal? We can turn to email and phone marketing to follow up.

AIDA Model

The letters in the AIDA model stand for **Awareness, Interest, Desire, Action.** It's shown in the form of a funnel since each phase follows the previous one and only a certain amount of the target audience advances to the next phase. The AIDA model isn't quite so popular today, yet it's suitable for planning advertising campaigns. Each phase requires a different approach to communication because the customers are in different decision-making stages and require different information to move on to the next step.

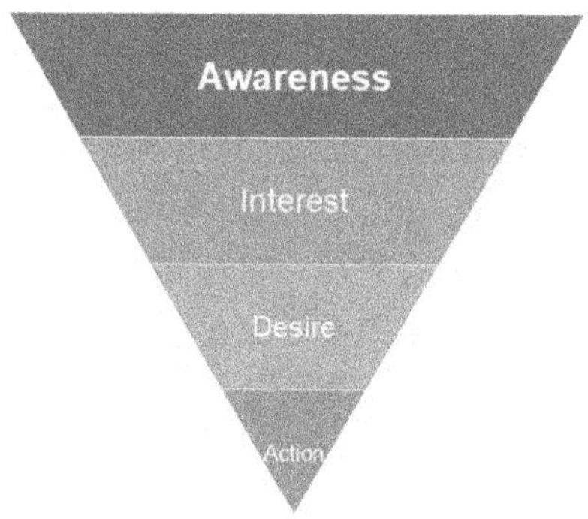

Phase 1: Awareness-building will be centered around TV ads, billboards, or banner ads. At this stage, the potential client has no reason to communicate with us, so we must start the conversation by getting them familiar with us.

By phase 2, there will be some people interested in our product or service, but not yet convinced they want to make a purchase. Or maybe they know they want to buy a certain product but are deciding between purchasing with us or our competition. This target audience needs information, reviews, comparisons – they want to know if they can trust us.

The **Interest** phase must be tailored to our store or webpage. The client wants to know more and is looking for fast information. Multiple pages with unclear information, documentation in another language, unclear prices, or difficult navigation reliably send customers to the competition.

By phase 3, **Desire,** the client wants to buy a product from us, and it's up to us to close the deal. Pay attention to both technical and marketing details. For example, can a client purchase without setting up an account? Can they pay by card? Are there options for how their goods will be delivered? What are the conditions for returning or exchanging items? Use tools that measure various steps of the pre-purchasing phase, so you can see where you might need to optimize.

The final phase, **Action,** is about achieving a specific goal. There may be some overlap with the previous phase. Goals can be defined in different ways – for example, opening an account with an online store, making a purchase, downloading a catalog. The AIDA model can also be used for smaller campaigns that don't cover the entire process. If you want people to subscribe to a newsletter, the action phase will be complete when they provide their email address and actually sign up to receive your newsletter.

The critics of the AIDA model point out that it's overly simplistic and doesn't include anything after the purchase (or applicable **action.**) Like any tool, marketing models have advantages and disadvantages. I recommend combining and adapting tools to your specific situation.

In this way, it's possible to give a skilled marketer structure without tying their hands creatively.

Taking Care of Clients Is The Most Powerful Form of Marketing. A story.

The previous chapter described the STDC model, where the C stands for "*care*". Many companies use marketing to lure in new customers to their store or website, but neglect to pay proper attention to the "*care*" step. By contrast, some entrepreneurs are very friendly with their clients and do some great marketing work without even realizing it.

One Friday night, I dropped my phone and cracked the screen. I did a quick internet search for repair options, found an ad with good reviews, and called the number. I agreed with the man who answered the phone to meet Saturday morning. I drove to the agreed-upon meeting place and gave him a call. He told me to go to the coffee shop across the street, order a drink on him, and wait until he arrived. I had a drink and waited for a couple of minutes. When he arrived, he took a look at my phone and told me he could fix it back at his phone repair shop. He hadn't mentioned in his advertisement that he owned a shop selling and servicing mobile devices. I didn't want to take up more of his time, so I thanked him for coming to meet me on a Saturday, and told him I would just go home and repair the cracked screen myself. He stopped me right away, saying he couldn't just let me leave without knowing that my screen was working again. It was a very kind approach. We walked back to the coffee shop, had coffee, he changed the display for me, and everything worked well. I bought some additional accessories in his shop, and he immediately offered me a discount.

I was very pleased about my shopping experience with this entrepreneur. After arriving home, I wrote him a positive review. Even though it's been several years, I still remember the experience and recommend his store to everyone.

Marketing and advertising campaigns can be copied from successful ones, but not every business will handle caring for their customers in the same way. There is always room to differentiate. Care is the most important factor in a good business relationship. Selling once is easy, but selling again and again requires business well-done.

I recommend thinking about *"care"* from the STDC model in detail and having a clear vision for how your company will enact it. When the *"care"* aspect of selling is well managed, other aspects of marketing will work much more effectively and the competition will be lost.

Predictably Irrational

Dan Ariely wrote a great book called *Predictably Irrational*. The author describes various social experiments and points to the irrational behavior of people. As amusing as this irrationality can be, it also has useful applications in marketing. We can use these insights to our advantage. Each psychological phenomenon can be viewed for its marketing impact – potential to sway customers into behaving in a way that benefits us. Alternatively, as customers, we can better avoid being taken in by advertising campaigns. I leave it to my readers to responsibly determine the boundary between suggestion and manipulation in their marketing endeavors.

Absolute Price And Relative Price Perception

People, in general, are not particularly perceptive about the absolute value of goods in different quantities. We need to have some relative metric at hand to be able to compare different values to something that we understand the value of. For example, heights and weights of a normal human are something we can readily make a relative comparison of. We can confidently say that 15 feet is tall compared to the average height of a person. We know that 200 pounds is more than we can carry in our hands. We can handle walking a mile if we have 30 minutes to get from point A to point B.

Comparing prices is more complex and the relative metrics are not always clear. One criterion we use is our income, but this number isn't always suitable. If the price of the goods accounts for only a fraction of the total income, then we know that we can afford to buy it, but we can't say whether it's cheap or expensive for what it is.

For example, when we buy cosmetics in a brick-and-mortar store, we usually compare the price across different brands. If we manage an online store with only one brand, we don't want the visitor to go compare with another website – we risk them not returning to our webpage. So, how can we solve this problem? Offer a way to compare prices within the brand offered!

Examples of creating a relative comparison. For cosmetics, we can work with different volumes or items. For example, when the price of a product is $5, it's difficult to assess whether it's too much or not. The customer will be a little confused and go looking for a comparison. We should offer it to them upfront! Perfume, 1 fl oz ml for $5. 2 fl oz instead of $7. The customer can see clearly that buying a larger amount will get them better value for their money.

Another option is to offer a package deal: Perfume, 1 fl oz for $7, or a duo-pack of perfume and hand lotion for $10.

Customers want to have the feeling that they've scored a deal. This is true even when the customer already knows they are going to buy something. If they already know they want product X from brand Y, being able to see that their purchase was justified by having a relative comparison to look at makes them feel satisfied and confident. I always recommend this strategy to my retail clients.

Price comparisons can be even more sophisticated if you sell more expensive goods and want to guide the client to the most expensive model. This works well for electronics, cars, and even real estate.

 **Example**. We sell televisions and have found that a given customer is willing to spend between $800 and $1,000. Our sales

goal is to get them to see the $1,000 model as having the best value. If we're especially talented, we may be able to convince the client that an even more expensive model is a better fit. At the same time, we want to prevent the client from leaving with the cheapest TV. How can we accomplish this?

First, we select a model that we know will fit the customer's requirements. Let's consider $950 as a price point. If we only offer the client one model, it will be embarrassing. Exalting the benefits of our chosen model will not help. The client doesn't have a scale by which to achieve the sense of *"I made a great purchase"*. To encourage this end-state, we should provide at least two more models with a lower and higher price point. Compare the models for the client by highlighting the advantages of the selected model over the cheaper model. For example, integrated internet connection, playback, 100-movie hard drive, and so on.

Knowing that the customer doesn't want to spend more than a thousand dollars, highlight the value of a model on the higher end on their price threshold. It's also important to include a higher price-point model, for example, at $1,200 to emphasize the comparative sufficiency of the recommended model. In practice, it works like this: *"The model I would recommend has all the features you need at $950. It has internet, a hard drive, multichannel sound, etc. By contrast, the next model up, for $1,200, doesn't offer much extra. There's a little bigger drive that you probably won't use, and a faster processor, but the performance is almost indistinguishable."*

We have created a comprehendible comparison in both directions for our client. The model we recommended is much better than the cheaper one, but at the same time, it's as good as the more expensive one. Now the client can make their purchase feeling that they have chosen well and gotten a good value.

A similar strategy in the service industry requires a much more creative approach, as there are significantly more options available. Similar services vary between different vendors, both in price and how they are carried out.

Example. In personal training, we can create a follow-up comparison. A typical session with a certified personal trainer costs between $50-100 for an hour. The price only covers the session. By contrast, our $150-per-hour service includes the sessions, plus email support, questions and answers, and a 100-page e-book on personal physical development.

The possibility of price comparison is very beneficial. We should remember that when it comes to such personalized services as personal training, counseling, tutoring, or advising, the client is buying our personality and time with an expert over just whatever service we are offering. It's best not to compete by price – compete by offering the benefits of working with you and the value of the results you can help your client achieve.

Evaluating Our Products

In my work as a marketing consultant, I have come across a difficult task that cannot be avoided. This is informing my clients that their product is not nearly as fantastic and exceptional as they might uncritically believe it to be. Frequently, clients know very little about their direct competition, and even less about their indirect competition.

In his book, Dan Ariely describes an experiment in which the winners of tickets for a sports game were asked to rate their tickets. Tickets were acquired through a lottery system in which a few people won, and the rest didn't receive anything. As part of the experiment, groups were asked how much they would be willing to pay for the tickets. Among the group who didn't win the tickets, the average price they were willing to pay was around $150. On the other hand, those who already had tickets were looking to sell them for approximately $1,500. There was an enormous difference in the perception of how much the tickets were worth based on the experience of getting or not getting the tickets. How could such a large difference in perceived value come about?

The ticket winners had an emotional experience that raised the value of the tickets in their eyes. Whether we are selling tickets, a bike, a car, or a house, it's not *just a thing* for us. We view our own experiences and emotions as part of the value of the material item. The value of the items grows for us based on how long we had it and how much it meant to us. On the other hand, the buyer sees only the object as it is. And although they may want the item, their price cap is going to be lower than that proposed by the seller. This is evidenced by the ticket experiment. An exchange only takes place when both sides can come to a compromise.

The second consideration in the perceived difference of value is a fear of loss on the part of the seller. We don't like to give up things we have a relationship with. I remember one neighbor who cried when selling his old car, even though he already had a new car parked in his garage. Even old, unnecessary, or broken things can be hard for some people to give up. The idea of loss aversion is one we will return to later in this book.

The third source of difference in value perception comes from the work put into acquiring the item in the first place. IKEA, for example, greatly benefits from this as actually assembling the furniture plays a part in their buyers' experience. People have a much stronger relationship with a wardrobe they built with their own hands than one that came to them pre-assembled. An old car is another example of this principle. While someone might look at your old car and see a piece of junk, its owner sees all the years of work repairing and maintaining the car in working order.

As marketers, we must ask ourselves how we can apply this principle to work in our favor. In car dealerships, the test drive is an example of this and a very important factor in making the sale. They want their potential customer to sit in the car, feel the seats, press the buttons on the dashboard, feel the car driving, experience the joyride. The longer the customer spends in that state, the more they already feel like the car belongs to them, and the stronger the need to buy it becomes. IKEA is another great example with their cozy showrooms that you have to walk through before getting to the store or warehouse. Yogoterie also uses a similar principle for selling frozen yoghurt. Customers take a cup and serve themselves any combination of yogurt flavors their hearts desire, then add fruits, candies, and nuts. The customer gets their dessert exactly the way they like it. People are happier with an outcome when they pour their creativity and effort into it. For them, it's special.

Good marketing communication can strengthen the vision of product ownership that ultimately leads to sales. It's important to demonstrate how it will feel for the customer to unpack and begin to use a product at home. For a sportscar: incredible views of the surroundings and a feeling of exceptionalism. For food: the texture and taste, the artful plating. For tickets to a music festival: the extraordinary ambiance and like-minded new friends.

If you can offer customers a chance to try your product for free and return it in a week, do it. The customer builds a relationship with the item once it's in the house, reducing the potential for returns, while at the same time loosening the customers' resistance to spend the money in the first place.

Loss Aversion

Loss aversion is an interesting example of perceiving reality in different ways. It's easy to confirm this phenomenon experimentally: toss a coin, if it lands on heads, give your friend $5, if it lands on tails, your friend gives you $5. There is an equal chance of winning or losing, but people tend to see the potential of losing $5 as more expensive than the possibility of gaining $5. That's not all. If you want to try this with your friends, ask them how high the winnings would have to be to justify the potential loss of $5. For some people, the possibility of winning $10 justifies betting $5, but for others, even a 3:1 ratio will still seem too risky. Amounts of $5 or $10 are modest, but increase the value to $5,000 or $10,000 and willingness to bet at a 2:1 ratio decreases even more.

To put it simply, people are afraid to lose what they have, even if they could potentially have more. How does this apply to marketing? Well, it's a bad strategy to put the customer in a position where they have to give something up. This could be exchanging one service provider for another, for example. To avoid the feeling of loss, people tend to cling on to what they have, even if they are missing out on potential benefits.

Typical examples of how to capitalize on the loss aversion phenomenon are limited-time offers: *"30% off, this week only!"* or *"Last pieces in stock!"* These have been over-used to the point that they have lost some influence, but the principle still works.

 **Example.** When preparing a marketing campaign, we try to think of ways to use loss aversion differently. One way is to

evoke in the client an atmosphere of what could happen if they miss out on the offer. Property damage in the case of insurance, or higher loan payments if they don't take advantage of favorable interest rates now.

Keep Options Open

Do you know the story of how Hernán Cortés conquered 16th century Central America? When they arrived in modern-day Mexico, Cortés ordered all ships to be burned. He told his people there was no turning back to Europe–they would either have glory or they would die trying. Chinese Commander Xiang Yu used a similar tactic around 230 BC. The soldiers had no choice but to fight as hard as they could. These leaders knew that people generally like to keep as many options open for themselves as possible. By destroying alternative options, they gained an army with no choice but to forge ahead.

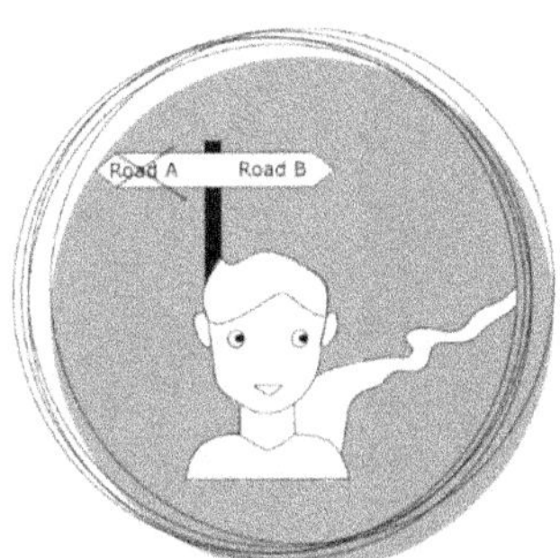

Nowadays, the human mind is much the same. We prefer access to as many options as possible and are reluctant to choose any path that would reduce the possibilities available to us in the future. Loss of options may not be forever. For example, the purchase of a car we will drive for some time, or a house we will live in for several years. Making a decision that will limit our options in the near future can cause stress and uncertainty.

Example. My college roommate wanted to buy a DSLR camera, and his first price cap was about $400. Then he examined what features were available and suddenly needed to have functions that *"might possibly be useful sometime in the future"*. In the end, he opted for a camera worth $750 – almost double his original cap!

We all know a story like this and have probably been equally as guilty of increasing our requirements to meet some hypothetical future demands. In short, we want to feel like we are prepared for any situation. The more options we have available as add-ons, the greater our imagination of scenarios in which we may use them, and the more drawn we become to the more expensive model.

This is especially true when it comes to purchasing a computer. The sheer number of options can be dizzying: What processor speed, how much memory, what disk size and video card performance, and so on. We start with one combination, then see that a better video card will increase the price *"only $25!"* Then we look to the processor, and a more powerful one is just an extra $30. We carry on with this until we realize that we've doubled the original price we set for ourselves. Now we're fighting with our emotions because we've created the combination we desire. The rational argument, that we really don't need such a high-performance device for what we're planning on using it for, somehow isn't a compelling argument. A few days later, we have our new computer sitting on our desk, packed full of features we will never take advantage of, but we're happy to have the machine designed according to our preferences.

Another typical example is modern marketing with numbers. When it comes to cell phones, camera resolution is one way for models to overtake each other in popularity. It's not exceptional to have a phone with an 18 MPx capability today. Technically, such a resolution is nonsense, because the simple optics of the mobile never match the large and expensive optics of a professional camera. Phone cameras generate folders worth of pictures with low quality but huge file size. These file sizes are automatically reduced when uploaded to social media anyway. In short, the high resolution of phone cameras doesn't make sense, but it has nevertheless become one of the marketing numbers to which customers respond.

How Our Expectations Shape Reality

Throughout this book, I have stressed how people perceive the reality around them in different ways. That which we observe isn't as obvious as we think it is, and everything becomes relative. Our reality is shaped by certain assumptions we carry that will color the resulting picture. It can be surprising to discover that someone next to us is looking at the same thing we are but seeing something completely different. This is because we, as humans, are not just information uploading machines. Sensory experiences arrive in the brain and are immediately joined up with existing records of previous experiences. One person looks at a bike and sees a great piece of exercise equipment, while someone else shivers, remembering a terrible accident they had in the past. Same thing, completely different perception.

We're familiar with the placebo effect from the medicine. The putative healing effects of a pill will affect our psyche so powerfully that our health will improve, even in the absence of active biochemical compounds.

Example. The variety of perceptions can be demonstrated by examining subjective categories such as tastes, sounds, and smells. Price-perception surveys show that our assumptions about these properties are extremely important in shaping the real experience. A group of people was provided with three samples of the same wine. They were told that the first sample was the most expensive, the second was mid-priced, and the third was cheap wine. The results show that most people rate what they thought was the most expensive wine as their favorite. The cheapest was rated as least popular. This experiment has an additional interesting moment. The experimenters added a bit of vinegar to the "most expensive" wine to degrade it, yet still, people came up with the same evaluation. Once again, people rated the "most expensive" wine as the best tasting, despite the additional vinegar most certainly degrading the objective taste.

To take advantage of the phenomenon of assumptions, we should think about things from the customer's point of view. What are they associating with our product? Maybe they are perceiving that a higher price represents a higher quality? Perhaps they are considering a specific parameter as a deciding factor? Perhaps the range of options available is critical? We can only get the answers to these questions by actively communicating with our client base. Clients can tell us everything. If we listen carefully and adapt, we can succeed.

One important warning here: While it's true that we can use marketing to evoke all sorts of positive emotions, watch out for unfulfilled promises. If you suggest to a customer that their trip will be to a lovely beach with sparkling blue water, they should not, in fact, have a trip to a dirty hotel with unpleasant staff. Disappointment is the worst result in marketing and business.

The Principle of Diminishing Sensitivity

The principle of diminishing sensitivity describes how people perceive numbers of different sizes – whether in price or quantity of goods. Put simply, customers see the difference between $10 and $20 as being larger than the difference between $100 and $110, even though the amount is the same. The principle of diminishing sensitivity points out people's weakness in perceiving absolute numbers – we prefer to have a comparison. We don't know how to think about that $10 on its own, so we need to compare it to other numbers.

The principle of diminishing sensitivity works nicely for expensive products. It's far easier to sell accessories with a car than it is to do so later. Designer mats for $300 will seem less expensive on a receipt next to a new car. Selling electronics, cars, jewelry, or furniture is always an opportunity to sell additional accessories. Once the customer is in the position of making a purchase, they are more open to buying additional items. This is called *"up-selling"*.

Up-selling is everywhere. When buying shoes, the salesperson will always suggest protective spray or leather crème to go with them. In women's clothing stores, the checkout counter typically has a jewelry display that the staff can refer the customer to before finishing payment. Obtaining the first *"yes"* to a sale makes receiving the next one much easier.

Anchoring

Anchoring is a cognitive distortion of the decision-making process whereby one source of information (usually the first we're exposed to) becomes the *"anchor"* of our opinion. It may only be an idea rather than objective information. Again, we follow up on the chapter on the need for relative comparison. Anchoring allows us to have a relative measure at hand.

Example. A typical example of anchoring is the difference between an employee's salary and the price of a service. For example, an employee receives payment as their net salary after paying taxes. There are no additional costs.

In contrast, a company or self-employed person receives money not as payment, but as turnover. They are obligated to pay taxes and levies, as well as time off, utilities, rent, and so on. For employees, making $30 an hour is quite fine. However, it wouldn't even be worth doing business for a company to get the same payment for an hour of work. The same work, for which the employee receives $30 in net would be invoiced by a company for $100 per hour. It seems like a huge difference at first glance.

Now, back to anchoring. The image you want to hire a company to build a fence around your house. You have never purchased a fence before and are unsure how much it will cost. You imagine you can do it yourself in about 20 hours, and so take your hourly salary and multiply it by 20 hours to get a price estimate. As you begin sending in inquiries to companies, you'll be shocked to find that the price comes back several times higher than your original thought. People can be slow to overcome their anchored view of how much they believe a fence should cost.

The anchoring effect can take many forms. For example, a potential client may focus on one part of our service that they can evaluate and not take into account other important components. This phenomenon occurs when someone orders a website. The visual component, the actual page, is what the client will think about, not taking into account the programming that goes into creating it. When a webpage needs more complex functions, like managing inventory, the presentation may be trivial, but the background functionality is crucial. Google is a great example – the main page is just a textbox but behind it is technology worth billions of dollars.

The problem that arises with anchoring is confirmatory distortion. People want to be right in their opinions and tend to be unwilling to change. Of course, we also want to confirm the opinions that we hold without objective information.

In marketing, anchoring is used alongside relative comparisons. A typical example of this is discounts. Many customers are not interested in the real value of an item, but the relative difference between the original price and the discount. Sometimes there is an absurd use of discounts because they work to convince customers to buy.

Example. Some companies gradually raise their prices before the discount season. After sales are announced, customers see a 20% discount on products that were priced higher a few weeks ago. Stores are occasionally caught doing this by shoppers who closely compare prices. For most people, however, discounts work reliably well. You can find even more examples of this online, which can either be an inspiration or a reminder of all the marketing tricks we are subjected to on a daily basis.

The Barnum Effect[16]

For decades, psychologists have researched human behavior and the various effects that accompany the decision-making of groups and individuals. Knowledge of these effects can help marketers understand the behavior of their clients and use it for effective sales strategies. The level to which you wish to use this psychological understanding is up to you as an individual, because it can quickly delve into the realm of manipulation.

American psychologist Bertram Forer[17] conducted a well-known experiment with a group of students. He asked them to complete personality tests that were supposed to characterize the true nature of a person. The test, however, was not evaluated. Forer gave all the students the same personality profile result and then asked them to evaluate the accuracy of the test on a scale of 1 to 5, where five meant absolute compliance with reality.

---

[16] Also called the Forer Effect
[17] en.wikipedia.org/wiki/Barnum_effect

"The results" of the test looked something like this:

- ♦ You have a great need for other people to like and admire you.

- ♦ You tend to be self-critical.

- ♦ Safety is one of your main life goals.

- ♦ Some of your aspirations tend to be unrealistic.

Take a look at these messages. Are you able to see yourself in them? In most cases, the answer is *yes*. This was also the result of Bertram Forer's students, who rated the results with a mark of 4.26 of 5 (i.e. highly accurate).

The joke lies in a very general wording of a message that most people can identify with. This is also the reason why horoscope, signs, oracles, numerology, and dream interpretation work. You can't go wrong!

Example. I once attended an event with a presenter who was an expert on deciphering the Mayan calendar. He told the crowd that this was a good month for travel. In the next sentence, he predicted that travel may not always work out, and gave an example of how he missed the bus.

What's interesting about this story? It precisely applies the Barnum effect. Things either work out or fail. This is a tautology – an always true statement. There is no other option.

How to use the Barnum effect in marketing?

Understanding this psychological principle will allow us to use it effectively, while at the same time, make us able to recognize when someone is using it against us. Let's do a quick summary. People aren't very critical of each other, they always want to feel the hope that things will go well (ideally effortlessly), they want to be seen positively in the eyes of others, not have to think too critically, and make a memorable first impression. People want to believe that every positive thing said about them is true. Getting praise always feels good, even when we know deep down that it's flattery.

We can use the Barnum effect to gain a specific group of people as our clients. We will create a positive characteristic of this group so that it's distinct from other groups. Then we highlight some very positive characteristics that are true of members of this group. So far, this is general advice, since for each group, we will need to use a different type of communication.

Examples:

"We're looking for the brightest programmers to join our team."

"By buying into this fund, you will be a member of an elite group owning a share of the most successful companies."

"The smartest homeowners use this service because..."

"We only insure good drivers!"

Follow ads and marketing messages around you to see how often you find such general claims. Nowadays, it's very important in marketing to find a reasonable level of manipulation, as customers are more resilient and mindful of new techniques than ever. When overused, this technique becomes nonsensical and its detection will have a negative effect.

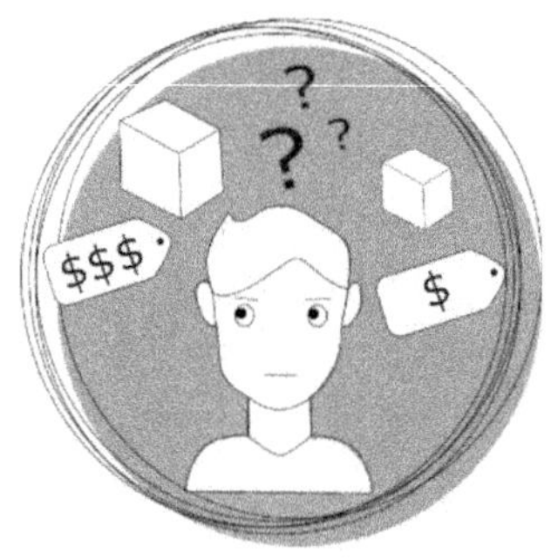

I Don't Know What I Want, I Know What I Don't Want

When talking with my clients, business partners, and even with young children, there is a noticeable pattern of people formulating their desires in the negative. They don't say what they want but rather focus on what they don't want. A job seeker might say: *"I don't want a stressful work environment. I don't want to do activities A, B, or C."* A client ordering a webpage might say: *"I don't want the page to be boring."* A customer getting their hair cut at a salon might say: *"Don't make it too short!"*

The trouble with only defining what we don't want is that it still leaves numerous open possibilities, not all of which we necessarily want. Our brains are not great at processing negative demands. This is most obvious in children. Tell them not to do something, and suddenly it becomes all they can think of.

The brain works with ideas and images. When someone tells us what not to do, our brain can't help but visualize it, even as we carry out the activity we should be doing. And in some cases, the idea tempts us so much that we succumb to it, however dangerous it may be.

Inexperienced marketers use negative claims too often because they focus solely on the product and not on the client. When was the last time you purchased goods or services because of *something it wasn't*? You don't buy a sports car because it isn't a minivan, but because you like the sleekness of the car. You don't buy more expensive snacks because they *"aren't made of potatoes"*, but because they taste good. At a software firm, I came across the slogan *"We're not just programmers."* Great! We know what you're not – so then, what are you?

Negative messages are less comprehensible and there are no clear benefits in using them. A person who just briefly views our website or billboard has no time or desire to think about *what we are not* at any depth. At the moment we have their attention, we should use it to evoke positive feelings and support associations leading to a better memory of our brand and content.

Social pressure and trying to fit in

Numerous social experiments demonstrate the power of social pressure. People don't like to be too different from those around them, and the pressure to fit in can cause strange behaviors.

One great social experiment is available to watch on YouTube[18]. The scene takes place in the waiting room of a doctor's office. The actors are told to all stand up when they hear a bell ring. The only one not informed is a girl who is being filmed by a hidden camera. She soon begins to stand up at the sound of the bell like the others, without knowing why. She continues standing up at the sound of the bell, even after the others leave the room – the social pressure is gone but the action has become a habit. After a while, new people arrive and begin standing at the sound of the bell themselves.

Succumbing to social pressure can very easily be used positively and negatively. It's up to everyone to know how to set the limits of

---

[18] Search for *Social Conformity* – Brain Games

manipulation. It's good to know about these techniques, especially in case someone tries to use them on us.

In marketing, social pressure and fear of exclusion from the group can be a powerful motivator. Children and young people, in particular, are noticeably sensitive to their status and acceptance within a group. If you're marketing to a younger audience, think about how to position your product as an important factor for social interaction. Marketing campaigns may suggest that your product can ensure more friends, higher status, greater popularity, and better experiences. The reverse can also be used – creating a fear that not having a given product will result in exclusion and loss of status. I personally endorse using a positive perspective, but it must be said that fear is an effective tool for manipulating people. Pay attention when someone tries similar tactics on you.

An important factor to consider is the theory of the diffusion of innovations and the specific group we are talking to. When we want to sell to innovators, then we're dealing with positive messages. We want the client to be first, innovative, unique. We sell diversity, performances of betrayals. Innovators always want to be different and are willing to pay premium prices to feel this way.

When we're using marketing to target a product to the majority, then we can include phrases such as, *"this is the product all your friends already have, what are you waiting for?"* or, "Hundreds of people are experiencing better health thanks to this product."

Many young people are on Facebook simply because their friends are there, and organize parties and various events through it. Those who don't have Facebook won't find out about the event. The social pressure and fear of missing out are what brings many people to social networks.

Cognitive Ease

Cognitive ease is a general measure of how easily our brain processes new information. There are several particular phenomena unique to humans, and knowledge of them will allow us to better work with information, avoid typical mistakes, and use them in the preparation of marketing communication.

♦ People find comfort and safety in what is familiar.

♦ Thinking takes energy and sometimes people would rather not have to think.

♦ People preferentially confirm what they already believe rather than look for a new perspective that could change their minds.

♦ A simple statement is perceived as true more often than a complicated one.

♦ The Halo Effect – people tend to make broad generalizations about things based on impressions. A symptom of the Halo Effect can be perceiving the world in terms of black and white.

Let's look at these phenomena individually, outside of the context of marketing. Think about how to use them to your advantage or eliminate their potentially negative impact.

Safety in familiarity

The fact that we feel more comfortable with what is familiar is intuitive but often overlooked. This is highlighted whenever a new product is introduced that has the potential to change society. Skepticism is often the first response to major novelties – airplanes, telephones, computers, tractors, the sewing machine. Great ideas may seem pointless at first, but only the market can test what consumers really think about a new product. For example, when developing text messaging, it was thought that no one would write a message when they could call instead. Skepticism about the usefulness of text messages resulted in the low character limit. However, users have fallen in love with texting and millions of texts are sent every day.

Sometimes, great ideas are not immediately accepted by the market for various reasons. Microsoft launched tablets in 2000, but they weren't particularly successful. At the time, mobile internet wasn't yet widespread, social networks hadn't become mainstream, and most people didn't have any reason to purchase such a relatively expensive device. It was too many new things at once. The success of tablets started in 2010 with the Apple iPad. The timing was much better. Wi-Fi and mobile internet were more available and social networking was in full swing. A compact tablet became desirable for many more customers. The functions and applications were familiar to users and so they gained market popularity.

Thinking takes energy

Thinking and deliberating over new stimulus is energy-intensive for the brain and our body intuitively tries to conserve energy. The brain prefers familiar scenarios where it can quickly and subconsciously apply learned decision-making processes. By contrast, conscious thinking takes more time. Think back to the first time you rode a bike or drove a car. There were so many new factors to keep track of and the brain had to be alert to everything – monitoring every movement of your hands and feet while keeping your attention on the road ahead. After some experience, the process became automatic, and applying conscious effort was no longer necessary in knowing which foot to use for the brake or how to steer.

In marketing, it's good to keep in mind that people prefer familiar processes and are reluctant to deal with new information, the processing of which requires extra work on their part. When generating advertising or marketing communications, frame your message in a way that is familiar to the client. Make it easy for the potential client to find you. If communication is easy on the client, it's easier to gain attention. Of course, clients fall into different groups with distinct preferences and interests and it's useful to break these groups down and communicate with them in a more targeted manner. The larger the group of people, the more general our message has to be, and the less interesting it will be to any particular member of the group. It's easy to create an ineffective ad. Breaking down your clients into smaller groups is the key to modern marketing. Internet technology has made this a much easier task than ever before.

Example. There is a strong tendency in marketing communications to want to reach everyone. The fear of missing out on potential clients leads us to create overly general and boring content that doesn't effectively interest anyone. These messages are product-focused rather than client-focused. Client-focused communication is more difficult because each category of our clientele has a different motivation to buy.

Imagine you want to sell expensive body paint for cars. You want everyone and anyone to buy your product, so you only create general communication:

"Our paint protects your car."

"Your car will look great in our paint!"

Now imagine you want to create an ad only for owners of luxury brand cars. This limits the target segment, yet it's more likely to reach the ideal client. Example:

"Owners of luxury cars know how to take care of their loved ones. That's why they use paint XYZ."

"Are you the owner of a luxury car who likes to pamper their favorite ride? Our paint XYZ is the best you can do!"

We can create many creative versions of marketing communication targeted at luxury car enthusiasts. We can assume this audience takes good care of their cars. On the other hand, this type of communication makes no sense for people who see their car as just a vehicle to get them around and have little interest in automotive care and upkeep.

People prefer to confirm what they believe rather than look for a new perspective and change their minds

As previously mentioned, people consider the information they have heard before to be safer and treat new information with distrust. It's easier to accept your current set of beliefs than it is to subject them to critical scrutiny. Some ideas have been passed on for so many generations that the origins can't be found.

Different sections of the population have different "truths" that are accepted without critical examination. Despite their untested nature, large groups of people will use these "truths" to make decisions, for better or for worse.

Before the Wright brothers' first successful flight, there was a general belief that objects heavier than air couldn't fly. The balloons were familiar, but few could imagine the plane. This "truth" made it very difficult for aircraft projects to gain support and funding.

One of the most successful marketing projects of all time was the De Beers campaign. In the 1930s, a diamond company launched an advertisement about the importance of a diamond engagement ring, which should ideally cost the groom two months' salary. Today, this superstition is taken as the standard and only a fraction of people know its origin. We must appreciate the genius of the campaign, which leaves traces in society even 90 years after its launch and affects shopping behavior to this day.

In the United States especially, patriotism is an attractive angle for marketers. It was a marketing campaign that launched eating bacon into an American tradition. Previously, bacon was an undesirable part of pork that no one was interested in. Now, bacon's place in a proper *"American breakfast"* is an established concept that few critically analyze.

When creating a campaign, consider whether we're attempting to make a change in shopping behavior, or contradict established habits and societal views in any way. These campaigns can still work but require time, effort, and a large budget. Moreover, people in different countries may react differently as a result of societal development, income level, religion, and culture.

Simple statements are accepted as true more often than complex ones

As previously mentioned, our brains save energy when they don't have to do conscious work. Thinking requires energy and many don't want to slow down and do the mental gymnastics. As a consequence, it's easier to take in and remember simple messages. Complex marketing messages or long slogans require effort to process and many people don't want to engage. Alternatively, the ad can appear at an inopportune time when the potential client simply doesn't have room in their brain to think about a complex message.

The general rule for advertising and marketing communication is to stick to general knowledge and communicate easily. For more complex messages, a blog, or product comparison site is more suitable. Especially advertising that targets new clients – do not waste time on technical details. The viewer or listener isn't yet willing to devote his energy to understanding a complicated message. This can be a problem when a manufacturer is proud of a technological solution but loses out on potential buyers by overexplaining details early on.

Halo Effect – the predominance of first impressions

The *Halo Effect* is an exceptionally powerful psychological effect that significantly influences our behavior and perceptions of reality. It lies in the fact that people take their first impression, whether positive or negative, and use it to judge other aspects of a person, product, or company.

Example. When looking at a photo of an unknown person, and that person is dressed up in either a suit or a fancy dress, we objectively know nothing about them. However, our brain quickly gets to work making generalizations by placing the image in a framework of what we already know. Good clothes usually pair with high income, status, and education or achievement. When random respondents are asked to estimate the income of a stranger, their answers vary widely depending on the clothing of the figure in question.

The Halo Effect has influenced marketing over the decades. Public opinion of brands is often tied to its historical success or failure. When a company conquers a product market, people will continue to perceive it as a reliable brand decades later, even if that evaluation is no longer correct. This works oppositely as well. When a company starts unsuccessfully, its bad reputation can prevent it from selling new products.

Personal marketing is very susceptible to the Halo Effect. When a client first interacts with us, labels like *"unreliable"* or *"doesn't respond to emails"* tend to stick. It can be hard to overcome our initial shortcomings. If our first impression is strong, however, clients will be more forgiving of later mistakes.

For our own marketing, whether corporate or personal, it's crucial to think about how we want the market to perceive us. Do we want to be serious, reliable? Or crazy, creative, and unpredictable? Possibly controversial or provocative? Once we choose our style, it stays with us. Any style can work, and we don't all need to wear a suit and tie. However, consistency is key.

Social Norms

In his book, Dan Ariely describes how social norms for personal relationships and commercial relationships differ significantly. When we do something for a family member or friend, we don't expect immediate reciprocity. Some things we do because we enjoy them, and some things we do as a way to help ourselves later on. Whether it's gifts, invitations to parties, or assistance with a move, we are will to offer or accept services without focusing on financial reciprocity.

Bringing money into social situations can be embarrassing. Imagine someone gives you a gift and you immediately give them something of equal value or even money. The gift-giver may feel a bit put off or offended. Money doesn't normally belong in social situations as it can create an unpleasant atmosphere for all involved.

In business relationships, money and financial remuneration have an essential place and all parties count on it. Problems arise when trying to combine social and business norms. Surely we have all had an experience where we tried to combine these approaches and created chaos. For example, paying for the lunch of a business partner.

Distinguishing between what is polite and expected depends a lot on society, the ages of the people, and cultural norms. Some customs that are common in the USA are unacceptable in Japan. Tips are a great example – it's considered obligatory to tip your waiter in the USA while in Japan, a waiter would run after you to return your money. It's considered impolite to accept more money than is stated in the menu price.

It's interesting in marketing how people evaluate the same thing in different circumstances. Imagine a neighbor contacts you to help them move some furniture. You agree in the spirit of common decency and good relations, or perhaps you want to do a good dead for someone. Now imagine the neighbor offers you $10 to help with the move. In this situation, you can easily compare the value of the reward with our normal salary. Our motivation can suddenly disappear. Even for the same situation, the circumstances change our perception and evaluation.

Remember that people, whether our clients or employees, will understand the same thing differently depending on the situation. Different emotions evoked by expectations, previous experiences, or even envy can enter into our perception. When we've accepted the task for an agreed reward of a hundred dollars, we can be completely satisfied. The moment we find out that a colleague received two thousand for the same task, we will be frustrated and much less motivated to give our best performance. This is the main reason why companies forbid employees to share wages. We mentioned that people generally have a very poor perception of absolute values and are always looking for relative comparison with something else. Social norms can be the source of comparison and the basis of what we take to be *"normal"* or *"fair"*. In the following chapter, we will show specific examples where social norms and commerce directly complicate business.

Selling With Compassion

In the social norms chapter, we stated that the context can significantly change the way a situation is perceived and, for example, affect the price that clients are willing to pay. During my practice, I met several start-ups that wanted to be socially oriented and at the same time benefit economically from their altruism. For example, a coffee staffed by individuals with Down syndrome. Problems can arise when social norms affect business transactions.

When a non-profit organization hosts a fundraiser to improve quality of life for individuals with Down syndrome, people are willing to contribute larger amounts of money. The social norm in this situation is to be selfless and give what you can. By contrast, when a business operates on a model based on employing people with Down syndrome, the context is now commercial. A person may be willing to donate $20 to a charity, but unwilling to pay $8 for a coffee just because part of the proceeds go to a good cause. When the customer is paying for a product or service, they are mainly interested in the perceived value of what they are receiving. All other considerations, including the social benefits, are secondary.

I often warn new start-ups not to go into a business like this with naivety. Being charitable can be complementary to the brand message, but it doesn't guarantee quality goods or services for the customer. A charitable business model alone isn't enough to sustain a successful company.

Keep in mind the value for the customer. If we address the customer's needs first – a good cup of coffee, for example – then the charitable aspect of the business can help form the story, and gain advertisement or media attention for free. But, if such a café only serves an expensive, yet underwhelming coffee, then no positive social message will save the business. The customers won't come. Clients may appreciate the socially forward aspect of the business, but may not want to regularly pay more for a cup of coffee. There are several such cafes in

Prague, which haven't been able to prosper despite considerable media attention. Initially, word spread fast and people were interested, but popularity declined as the service itself wasn't attractive to maintain a regular customer base.

Remember, the most important factor is the value for the customer. Everything else comes second and maybe complementary in certain situations. If the first condition is not met and the business is unable to satisfy a customer's needs, no other factor will redeem the business.

The Grass Is Always Greener

As the saying goes, *"the grass is always greener on the other side of the fence"*. People tend to be unsatisfied with what they have and focus instead on what others have. Modern society has only made this phenomenon more pronounced. This causes frustration at every choice. Whether buying a watch, a car, or a house, it's easy to fall into a cycle of doubt and anxiety about whether any given choice is the right choice. Paradoxically, the more choices we have to choose from, the stronger the negative emotions can be.

Satisfaction in one's life should be the goal of any endeavor. There will always be a more powerful car engine or a bigger house, but making comparisons is wasting energy.

Successful marketing invokes emotion, experience, and optimism about the future. Remember the idea that *"the grass is always greener on the other side"*. Create a clear idea for customers about how their lives will improve after they buy our car, come to our salon, or create their company website through our agency. Confront the customer with a vision of how their situation will be different after their purchase with us compared to their situation currently. Invoke curiosity, and make the customer do mental comparisons with their own life. When the customer feels we can help them improve an aspect of their life, they will come to us for our services.

Client Or Commodity

Currently, many services are available for free. This creates confusion over whether the user is the customer or the commodity. There are a few examples of this, but here I will only cover two major ones.

Social networks

Social networks are free to join, but their development and operation costs money. We know that social networks have their operating costs covered by advertising. We, the users, are not the clients of social networks, we are the product. Social networks entice us into spending time so that they can show us ads. Our attention is the commodity, along with our personal information, which can be valuable for marketing purposes.

The one who pays is the client.

The one who gets a service for free is the product.

How does this difference between client and commodity usually manifest itself? Well, if a user of social networks has a problem and wants to get help, it won't be easy. On the other hand, a paying client will have options to email or live chat, or have a ticket system where employees respond directly. Companies take care of their paying clients and spend as little time on the product/users as possible while still maintaining a profitable system.

Recruiting

Recruitment is a large industry. Let's examine the client-commodity relationship here. People looking for a new job don't always realize that recruitment agencies don't work for them, but for the companies that pay them.

Recruiters frequently deal with such reports from candidates:

◆ I'm unsatisfied with your service as you haven't found me a suitable job.

◆ You should find work for me.

◆ It's your job to find a place to employ me.

◆ I'm your client and I want feedback.

Those who don't pay for a service aren't the clients. Job candidates are commodities traded by agencies. The client in the company for which the recruiter fills vacancies. If a candidate wants someone to find them a job, it's a service that must be paid for. If a candidate gets this service for free, they're in no position to determine the conditions.

There's no disgrace in being a commodity. Both parties bring something of value to the relationship and everyone benefits. If no balance was found, the business model wouldn't work. One party brings money – the client – and they get to determine the conditions. They also benefit from customer support as part of the service. The other party brings time, information, skills, and labor. The second party still gets a certain service for free – getting to use a particular software or having the opportunity to interview for a job. However, this party isn't entitled to the same privileges and support as the paying client. Finding a new commodity is usually easier than finding a new client.

Bad Samples And Biased Selection

Statistics can be a demanding discipline in mathematics and not everyone has a fundamental relationship with them. Statistics, however, make for decidedly useful knowledge and a lack of statistical understanding will be reflected in one's understanding of reality. A fundamental rule in statistics is the need for a representative sample. What does this mean?

If we're interested in the preference of the whole population, we must have a sample in which the individual groups are represented at the same level as they are in the population as a whole. For example, it should be about half men and half women. If we want to know a general opinion, but only ask women, our data won't be reliable. Similarly, age, education, and other criteria should be taken into account.

We may have a non-random sample without realizing it at first glance. Take a pub – one that is a bit dirty, smokey, and serves cheap beer. The pub may attract regulars and they may praise it as being a great place to go. The owner of the pub may wonder why it's not more financially successful when everyone who comes to the pub seems to love it. As mentioned in the Positive Feedback chapter, the problem here is that the owner has fallen into a trap of a non-random sample. It's nice that existing customers are satisfied, but there aren't that many customers in total and the business isn't making money. In this case, it's necessary to get feedback from all potential clients, not only loyal return customers – a sample of all beer drinkers, or all those who enjoy spending evenings in pubs, not just those who don't mind a smokey atmosphere and cheap beer.

Watch out for hypotheticals

When obtaining data from potential markets or clients, watch out for hypotheticals. We can ask how people would imagine the ideal pub, but this may not be a reliable source of data. Many companies do extensive research before launching new products or services. They might ask, for example, what price point would be acceptable. This question is downright dangerous. The hypothetical "right" price is completely different from the price people will feel is appropriate in a given context. The market may react very differently if asked hypothetically than they will in reality.

Surveys, data collection, and analysis are all important aspects of a company's development. Statistics provide companies with tools to process the collected data. However, pay attention to assumptions, especially with surveys, and take care when interpreting results.

Dunning-Kruger Effect

Cognitive distortion can lead one to incorrectly evaluate their abilities in comparison with others. Usually, the less competent and capable a person is, the more likely they are to overestimate their ability. By contrast, the best in the industry tend to underestimate themselves.

The Dunning-Kruger effect makes it difficult to have frank discussions with incompetent people. It's useful to understand this phenomenon, especially if you lead a diverse team of people with different levels of competency.

One way to spot the Dunning-Kruger effect is to ask general questions related to self-assessment. Something along the lines of, *"Are you a good driver?"* or *"Are you a good cook?"* Often the response will be *"I'm above average"*, even if they are wildly incompetent.

Knowledge about the Dunning-Kruger effect can also be effectively used in marketing. We can assume that people tend to consider themselves above average. Therefore, generating marketing targeting to fix people's shortcomings may not be effective. People with poor eating habits don't want to be told that their way of doing things is wrong and they need the help of a nutrition and weight loss course. People who consider themselves singers don't want a company to tell them they lack natural talent and would benefit from a course. As previously mentioned in the chapter about the Barnum Effect, marketing should target a group to which consumers would like to belong. We can use the Dunning-Kruger effect to give people the impression that they already belong to such a group. Slogans like, *"we only insure the best drivers"*, and *"professional singers swear by our products"*, allow consumers to feel that by choosing a specific product, they already belong in the elite category. To capture this effect, think about what the ideal customer values, what their goals are, what they need to achieve them – then frame the product or service as a resource to support that goal.

Survivorship Bias

Survivorship bias is a logical fallacy that can cause people to draw incorrect conclusions from given assumptions. A famous example of this is that during World War II, the statistician Abraham Wald noticed that engineers were trying to improve the most damaged areas of airplanes that returned to the base. Wald realized that they weren't taking into account all the planes that had not returned to the base. By fixing the areas of the planes that were damaged after returning, they neglected to improve the weaker areas that led to some planes never returning at all.

In marketing, survivorship bias manifests in the positive feedback of current clients, not in the omission of clients who never came back. I already mentioned how even a bad restaurant or pub can gain loyal clients. It isn't enough to ask only our current clients. Valuable feedback comes from clients who tried a product or service and didn't return.

I also already mentioned the hype about Mark's Zuckerberg's grey t-shirt. This is another example of survivor bias. When a company is successful, people want to imitate their actions. People fail to account for all the other entrepreneurs who didn't make it. There is more to learn from mistakes than from success. Success stories can come from luck, coincidence, or a series of unlikely circumstances. Some people then attempt to attribute success to completely unrelated actions or decisions. Survival bias is closely related to the Skinner experiment on superstition, which can be found in an earlier section of this book.

Whenever collecting a satisfaction questionnaire, be careful to not only get answers from satisfied clients – the results will be positive but ultimately useless. Questionnaires often omit potential clients who either don't know the company or are put off by bad reviews or high prices. Data must be collected in a random and unbiased fashion and processed correctly using statistics. The alternative is deceiving ourselves into thinking our incorrect opinion is based on real measured data. This is a dangerous position. Many people go bankrupt rather than examine their opinions and attitudes at the expense of their ego.

Competition Versus Innovative Start-ups

We already discussed how not one of the large train companies became a leader in air travel at the start of the 20th century. These companies already had the clients, the budget, and the technical teams assembled. Their position was perfect to expand into new areas of transport. However, these companies chose to remain focused only on trains. They dealt with the product, rather than the solution for their clients. The clients were interested in traveling long distances in a short time. Train companies would rather attempt to make trains faster than expand their field and offer new products.

Even if you run a large and successful company, there is always a risk of being beaten by a start-up so small you never took notice of it. Big companies tend to look to other big companies as their major competition. Here are some interesting examples of how this went wrong.

Example. In the year 2000, Yahoo accounted for 50% of the internet search market. Google didn't even exist. Yahoo was worth billions of dollars while Google was created as a student project. The billion-dollar company didn't feel threatened by the unknown algorithms and instead kept its watch on Altavista. In a few short years, Google surpassed Yahoo.

A similar thing happened with Friendster and Myspace. They competed with each other and fought for users. Meanwhile, Facebook surpassed both of these companies. It wasn't long before Friendster and Myspace became stagnant and forgotten. In short, large companies lacked sufficient innovative potential despite their budgets and access to top professionals. Even the giant Google tried to break into the social network market with Google+, which ultimately failed and disappeared.

We've mentioned Nokia before, but it's a great example here as well. The corporation occupied 50% of the world market and was Apple's main competitor. Then the Korean company Samsung developed rapidly, made several excellent technological decisions, and rolled over Nokia in the smartphone market.

We could learn two key lessons from this chapter. The first is that success today doesn't guarantee success tomorrow, even though we currently occupy half the world market. The second lesson is that innovation doesn't require huge budgets, large buildings, and expensive company cars. It's looking for an idea that will improve the lives of a lot of people. Only then can we gain the attention of clients and investors who are happy to support us. On the contrary, a bad idea goes bankrupt no matter how much money investors bring in, as in the case of the billion-dollar WeWork start-up or the big scam company Theranos.

Personal Marketing

What And *Why* In Personal Marketing

Personal marketing is a way of presenting yourself. How do you want others to see you? What impression do you want to leave on them? What information do you want people to take away after meeting you for the first time?

People don't often think about themselves in the context of marketing. I would argue that this is necessary if you want to develop yourself and have better results in dealing with all people. Our personal presentation is reflected throughout our company and business relations. Business owners are often unaware of how much of an impact their personality and attitude have on their company.

We have already shown how important the question *why* is in marketing. The same approach is also essential in personal presentation and leadership. *What* we do may not distinguish us from others around us, but we can still be different from our competition. A marketing mindset can bring uniqueness and originality to the way we present ourselves and our business by giving a good answer to *why* and perhaps also *how* we do what we do.

When it comes to leadership, the importance of explaining *why* is even greater because we need to align our motivation with corporate goals and with the goals of our employees. When these three elements are not aligned, problems can appear in the form of misunderstandings, conflicts, bad marketing strategies, unfulfilled promises, bad service, and the like. Clients sometimes ask me how a company that looks very much like their own on the outside, can have much greater success. The difference is often lying in the alignment of personal and corporate goals, and their respective compliance.

Example. Let's take a restaurant as our model. The owner wants to create a fine restaurant and puts its focus on a great chef and a classy menu. They don't want to spend much time with the waitstaff, and only hire some part-time workers, who lack the necessary experience and have no idea about the restaurant owner's vision. We can probably already guess how this is going to work out. The service will always be inadequate to match the price tag on the menu, and the clientele willing to spend a significant amount for a night in an upscale restaurant will leave unsatisfied. The food prices will indicate high quality, but the clothing, behavior, and attitude of the wait-staff won't meet expectations. The restaurant will gradually lose clients and business will stagnate.

In the chapter on marketing processes, we will discuss this concept and how to build it up. The owner is always responsible for the direction of the company and they must communicate their goals to the staff. And not only that. It's necessary they hire employees who agree with the stated objective and will actively support the direction of the company.

When coming up with the objective of a company, it's important to answer as many *why* questions as possible. This will help us select the right staff and marketing direction for maximum success. Let's go back to the example of an upscale restaurant for a moment.

The role of the restaurant owner

Why open a restaurant? I have loved cooking my whole life and am constantly coming up with new recipes. I have traveled all over Europe tasting new and exciting dishes. I want to bring that experience to diners in my home country.

Why an upscale restaurant? The quality of the food must be accounted for in the price. I want to attract guests who appreciate exceptionally prepared, quality food and who aren't concerned with the price. I'm not simply creating a meal, but a gastronomic experience.

What do I want to achieve in my career and why? I want to show that cooking is an art. I want to participate in competitions and strive for a Michelin star for my restaurant. I want to be known among my clients and build name recognition, not only for my restaurant but also for myself. I also want to raise awareness about healthy food and great recipes.

I highly recommend writing out some similar answers as they apply to you and your situation. They will help you clarify both your motivation and the first steps on the way to fulfilling your vision.

The role of leadership

Successful companies aren't made without good employees, so you will likely find yourself in a leadership role. It's no longer enough to only have a vision. It's necessary you communicate that vision, both to your potential employees and your clients.

A restaurant will need waitstaff and a bartender with the same goal as the owner. The question is, *why* should they be interested in helping you fulfill your goal?

Again, we arrive back at answering the question of *why*. When recruiting new staff, if you explain your vision for the company, you can quickly see if the candidate will be an appropriate fit or not. The key messages in recruitment are as follows:

- We're creating an upscale restaurant **because** we want to cater to high-end clientele with good taste.

- Quality is essential **because** it's the only way to get paid more for a service, despite our competition.

- **Because** the quality of a well-known restaurant will attract high caliber guests, it will bring us stability in our business and income.

- **Because** we will be well known, we will have the opportunity to do more than just cooking – we will take part in competitions, social events, presentations, and even show business. The role of the chef or bartender has the potential to attract personal fame.

- **Because** we want to fulfill this vision, we need to pride ourselves on details. This means having top quality service, performance, appearance, clothing, products, and above all, customer service.

- **Because** we want to develop our name recognition, it will be necessary for employees to constantly work on personal development and educate themselves and others to be of the highest caliber.

When you communicate your values directly in this way, you can get immediate feedback from potential recruits. You can quickly see whether the applicant is interested in a serious career in gastronomy, or just looking for a part-time gig to make a little extra money. Don't be afraid to reject those who don't align with your concept and vision. Every element of a new company must be in support of the mission. Employees are among the most important elements.

In our next example, we will look at how bad management can lead to a high turnover rate. There isn't much difference between a poorly chosen staff and a great staff that is poorly managed.

Example. The owner of a new store achieved success in his business initially by building up clientele and gaining a steady stream of orders. He wants to enjoy the realization of his dream rather than deal with the day-to-day workings of the shop, and so hires the first person he can find to take care of the business for him. The owner isn't interested in dealing with people and doesn't put much stock in personal development. These are the results of his approach:

After a year of work, the newly hired employee doesn't bring a single new contract. The business owner maintains the position that it's not his responsibility to be a business teacher. He just wanted to hire someone and let the work take care of itself. This approach sends a clear signal to the employee that the owner isn't interested in their work or progress. As the employee continues to work without guidance or feedback, their enthusiasm for work wanes. They start to do the bare minimum amount of work necessary to keep earning a paycheck.

The story doesn't end there. Another employee is hired, this one of a completely different nature: younger and more enthusiastic. At first, it seems like a good choice. But unacknowledged work ethic and little success in the business, despite their efforts, means that this salesperson will soon lose their taste for work just like the previous one. The story repeats. Less work gets done, and eventually, the employees quit or are fired.

A third employee comes along, again completely different from the previous two. This one is an experienced businessman who previously ran his own company. Once again, despite the employee's efforts, the owner is unsatisfied with their performance and terminates their employment. The company has no choice but to return to the original model of the owner performing all functions in the business.

What is the common factor between these 3 diverse employees? The owner's personality and approach to business! Doing the same thing over and over again, the owner should not have expected different results. If something in business isn't working, it's always worth examining *"Can I, as the business owner, do something different?"* The answer is always **yes**. If it isn't clear what should be changed, it's perfectly advisable to hire external assistance in the form of a personal coach or business consultant.

In this story, the aim was to highlight the consequences of a bad approach, although the approach may initially seem fine. The owner wanted to hire a professional and get out of the way. This presented itself in the form of *"Do whatever you want, I'm only interested in the outcome."* This can also be interpreted as *"I don't care, I want results"*, which is one of the worst approaches to take when working with people. Disinterest is worse than negative feedback in most cases. The personal marketing of the owner failed, and with it, the management of their employees.

What could the owner have done better?

Above all, the owner could have showed interest in their personnel, and cared about the motivation and development of the employees. This is why it's useful to go through all those *whys* for the company and establish goals with the employees. The owner in the story could have achieved his goal of leaving employees to carry out their tasks, as long as he took the time initially to establish a good understanding of what the employees should be doing in his absence. Direct communication, business meetings, planning, preparation of marketing materials, and rehearsing conversation points for negotiations are extremely important tools in the development of reliable employees. People are generally reluctant to admit when they're unsure or need help, and it's up to management to establish employee-development initiatives.

Remember that simply setting a goal, such as getting more customers, or making more money, is meaningless without follow-up actions to help those goals become reality. Unless the employee knows how to fulfill the goals, they likely won't make much progress without additional input.

Am I Good Enough?

Parents often make one well-intentioned, but fundamentally misguided, mistake with their children. Their main goal is to protect their offspring from harm or disappointment. Parents simply worry about their children and want to protect them. Comments like, *"Don't run, you might trip and hurt yourself!"*, *"Don't climb that tree or you will fall!"*, *"You shouldn't go skiing, it can be dangerous!"* probably sound familiar from childhood.

What are these sentences saying, even though it isn't their intended purpose? They are emphasizing: **You're not good enough to be successful.**

We may carry this inner conviction with us throughout our life. When I meet with new clients for consultations, this usually comes up and the client realizes that they've been limiting themselves their whole life.

How can an emotion – fear – be so strong that it physically paralyzes us? The answer lies in evolutionary biology. For humans and other animals, responding to a false alarm is no big deal. If the sound of a branch breaking causes an animal to run away in fear, it's not a problem. Nothing harmful happened on account of the false alarm. On the other hand, the underassessment of danger can be very costly. From an evolutionary perspective, it's almost always better to run than it is to stand around waiting for more information – even a few moments of hesitation can have potentially deadly consequences. Moreover, the mammalian body is highly evolved to respond quickly to perceived danger. In a moment of danger, the heart rate increases, adrenaline floods the system, and the muscles become capable of explosive short-term performance.

Fear protects us, but it also limits us. The threat we're responding to doesn't have to be physical. We all remember the feeling before our first experience in public speaking: the sweaty palms, the shaky voice, the tightness in our stomach, and the pounding of our heart. The stress doesn't come from fear for our lives but from fear of what the audience may think of us. The brain has unlimited imagination and unfortunately can use that imagination to think through even the tiniest details of catastrophe scenarios. This brings fear from an imagined outcome, which, nevertheless, presents as genuine stress. Additionally, stress may cause us to act emotionally in scenarios where a bit more logic and thinking things through would serve the situation better. The physiological reaction of the body to psychological stress is the same as if there were a genuine threat to our lives. For the body, this physiological state of stress isn't ideal and can incur adverse health effects when experienced consistently over time.

Self-doubt and constantly questioning *"Am I good enough"* can be overcome through consistent effort. If you're concerned about your levels of self-doubt, it can be extremely helpful to schedule a few sessions with a personal coach to help you get out of your head. In the following sections, we will focus on how to see yourself with fresh eyes and work on your personal marketing.

Story. Let's take a short detour to see how to better lead children in healthy self-evaluation. Of course, we agree that parents have to do their best to protect their children from serious harm. When a child wants to try something dangerous for the first time, our knee-jerk reaction is likely to say, "*Don't do that, you could hurt yourself*". This reaction is simple because simply banning a child from an activity requires no further thought. However, always engaging in this reaction is harmful to the child's long-term development.

While on a trip to a popular rocky hiking destination outside of Prague, I witnessed an excellent example of how parents can create an educational experience for their child. A little girl – maybe three or four years old – wanted to climb on the rocks. The parents behaved calmly. The girl was given a helmet and her dad stood behind her with his hands, ready to catch her if she slipped. She climbed to four-times her height, a terrific performance for the young person, and had a great experience doing it. Then she wanted to come down.

The parents did a great job by actively guarding the girl's safety so that she could have a learning experience and gain greater self-confidence. This approach is highly valuable for children. Not only can they enjoy the experience in the moment, but they will carry healthy self-esteem and confidence throughout their lives.

The Difference Between Confidence And Arrogance

The words *confidence* and *arrogance* are often misused. We may incorrectly say that someone is *too confident*. So, what exactly is the line between these two traits? American therapist and public speaker, Sean Stephenson, presents a handy way to differentiate between self-confidence and arrogance. We'll use his analogy and build upon it.

Arrogance is about having something to prove. Arrogant people need to show those around them how great they are, or they need to prove it to themselves. Arrogant behavior stems from the fact that these people want a certain reaction from others—whether that be recognition, praise, or fame. The nature of this attention isn't necessarily positive; an arrogant person can find the result they are looking for even from the fear and hatred of others. In short, arrogance is about proving something and needing the acknowledgment of others.

Confidence relates to improvement. Confident people make decisions and engage in actions to improve the lives of themselves and others. They aren't looking for praise and awards to acknowledge their work. They don't always have to be in the front of photos. They don't have to manipulate others to behave the way they want them to. **They're interested in making things better.**

Arrogance and self-confidence are not the same thing, although they are often intertwined. The difference lies in self-awareness, and the individual's personal value system – regardless of the opinions of others. Confidence doesn't require outsider praise; it's built upon a person's vision of themself and their efforts to improve the world around them.

How others judge our decisions is irrelevant. The opinions of our family, friends, and acquaintances reflect only one thing – **how that person would act in our situation**. The views of others can be one way to gain an outside perspective. However, discussions turn unproductive when it comes to phrasings like, "do it like this," or "act this way". No one likes this type of communication. No one else has access to all the information we're using to make our own decisions. They aren't equipped to give us perfect advice because they simply aren't us. Advice may be well-meant, but without actual value regarding the decision before us. As we get older, we become more immune to phrases such as *"you must"* and *"you have to"* but we continue to use these phrases, especially with those younger than us. These phrases are a source of generational conflict between parents and their adult children.

Let's return to the difference between arrogance and self-confidence. I will give you an example from my life.

Example. For a long time, there was a man in a metro station who sold a charity magazine. Over time, he changed his attitude towards the people passing through on their way to work. He became increasingly rude and belligerent to those around him. He started yelling out things like, *"Look at you, too busy rushing to work to spare a glance."*, or *"Oh yes, heads down, how pathetic you all are!"*. After a while this person disappeared from the station, I assume due to complaints. He lowered the reputation of all other magazine sellers and, most of all, himself.

Would you label this behavior as arrogant or self-confident? We can probably agree this is arrogance. His goal was to manipulate those around him to pay attention. When it didn't work, he switched to aggression and swearing, which made his ability to sell anything even worse. I'm sure his version of the story would have involved self-important office workers, too busy rushing to work to make time for a poor magazine seller. Unfortunately, his attitude generally provoked resistance rather than compassion or interest in buying his magazines.

A Positive Example could be someone who busks in the metro station, playing guitar or violin. When they play music and enjoy themselves in the process, it adds value and makes the atmosphere better for those traveling in the metro. There is no manipulation or guilt in this act, and people aren't against giving a few coins. The musician's approach is one of self-confidence.

If you're wondering whether you come across as arrogant, you should consider your surroundings? Ask yourself: *"Do I add value?"* or *"Is my goal to improve my surroundings?"*. If you can answer yes to both these questions, then you're not being arrogant. Think about yourself a bit more. Consider what value your personality and approach are providing. This will give you a sense of self-awareness – **and self-confidence**. Being aware and conscious of your attitude and approach can give you greater peace of mind when presenting your work and communicating with clients and partners. When you know that your business is based on your values (quality, service, access, reliability), then you start to notice and appreciate these same aspects in others. You will automatically build closer, friendlier relationships that are economically valuable and make work more enjoyable.

The topic of self-confidence can be a stumbling block for many. *"If I focus on providing value and never act arrogantly, does it mean that no one can accuse me of arrogance?"* Unfortunately, the answer is **no**. When we work at our goals to live the life we desire and are creators of our own reality rather than victims of it, we will automatically attract attention from others. The more success we have, the more people will pay attention – including those who aren't happy for us.

People who have yet to find the courage and strength to change their lives for the better will take on the role of the victim. They may not be happy, but they're comfortable and don't want to change. At first, that last sentence reads like complete nonsense. *"they aren't happy"* and *"they are comfortable"*? How can they be both? The human brain deals with this contradiction through rationalization. You have likely encountered people with skeptical opinions, saying things such as, *"there's always a catch"*; *"they aren't telling us everything"*; *"no one makes that much money unless they are doing something illegal"*.

One of my clients worked very hard to build up her business. Some of her acquaintances spread nasty rumors that she must be selling her body, and other such nonsense to explain her success. It's ugly, but unfortunately, it happens routinely. It can be a frustrating experience for newly successful people. Old acquaintances may turn their backs and become unfriendly. Success requires a new perspective on life and a new approach to people.

How can we deal with *haters*, and avoid unnecessary self-doubt? One approach to our anti-fans is to welcome them. Success automatically attracts them. If we have no one to challenge us, we've probably haven't reached a high enough level yet, or no one cares what we're doing. We can't please everyone. There will be three groups: one which will support us, one which will take from us, and one which will hate us. Part of success is accepting the presence of all three of these groups as a positive indicator of our success.

In the following picture, we can look at the impossibility of pleasing everyone. Even in marketing, it's important to choose one target group and not worry about everyone else's expectations. Making everyone happy simply isn't possible.

From a marketing point of view, dividing the audience into fans and non-fans is beneficial. All social media likes, comments, and shares increase media visibility that we would otherwise have to pay for. More activity means more exposure for free. Discussions generated between our fans and non-fans will still increase our overall visibility. We can't eliminate haters – they will follow us, even if only to post snide comments. Since we can't get rid of them, we may as well use them to our advantage.

"You should..."

It's surprising how often we use the phrase "should" without thinking deeper about its implications. When we say *should*, we're expressing some contradiction between what we are doing and what someone else thinks we should do. It may sound complicated, so I will give some examples.

Example. Successful and unhappy. Even among extremely successful entrepreneurs, I have encountered people who were dissatisfied and frustrated with their current position. On the outside, everything seems perfect – they own their own company, they make a lot of money, and they have a great family. Outsiders consider them successful and don't understand what they could be dissatisfied about. They seem to have it all!

Our sense of happiness is completely removed from the opinions of others. Emotions result from internal beliefs and personal circumstances. For example, when a company grows rapidly, there are many reasons why the person managing it may not feel great – administrative tasks, the stress of coordinating staff, frequent travel. Exhaustion, frustration, and anger can easily build up. This situation often leads to the sale of the company. Many well-known start-up founders have discussed this.

Even if we're doing well and making money, we can feel like we want to be somewhere else. We may feel called to fight poachers in Africa, save whales, or build schools for the poor. Meanwhile, there will be pressure from those around us, telling us that we *should* do this or that. We can find ourselves gridlocked in uncertainty, which only increases the rate of burnout. Rationalizing our way out of our feelings doesn't do much good.

Example. Friends and family. Imagine that you have a decent job, you built a career for yourself, made good money, and now you want to go out on your own and start a business. People in your life may start to insist that *you should* earn more money, pay off your mortgage first, start a family, and not take on such a big risk.

We're all familiar with these comments, and no one particularly likes them.

I always stress to my clients that the opinions of friends and family shouldn't unduly influence them, as these people don't really know what they're giving advice about. The situation goes as follows. Aside from ourselves, no one can fully know our situation and all the history, emotions, and experiences that go along with it. It's impossible for the person giving us the advice to have all this essential past and present information at their disposal when they tell us what we should do. What is going on? When our loved ones try to advise us in good faith, they will create their own understanding of our reality. This person then places themselves in the imaginary reality and thinks about how they would act. Based on this, they start to give us advice. Think about a time you were in this situation. Did you come away thinking, *"That was some really apropos advice!"*? Or did you think to yourself, *"This person has no idea what they are talking about."*? Usually, it's the second option. We need to make our own decisions because those giving us advice are just deciding for themselves in a hypothetical situation.

How *"You should..."* really works:

- Someone creates an idea of our situation based on limited information.

- They put themselves in the situation they have created in their mind.

- They think about how they would act in this fictional situation.

- Based on themselves, they will say to you, *"you should do this..."*

Summary: If someone tells us what we should do, we can stop them right away. There is very little useful information in these uninvited counseling sessions. The other person won't tell us the right answer because they just don't know it. It's not worth worrying over and forcing ourselves to do things that we don't want to do. I also recommend you refrain from giving this same type of *"you should"* advice to others.

Toxic Personalities

It's been said that the average person has only five people who are truly close to them. These people can be family members, friends, or coworkers. Whether by habits, finances, or social status, successful people help us up, and unsuccessful or frustrated people pull us down. Although many young people have hundreds of contacts on social media, they only know a few dozen on a deeper level. We don't have the capacity for more close relationships, whether in terms of time or emotional capacity. It's important to choose friends who we will be able to dedicate our time and energy to. Many relationships are maintained out of certain inertia, sense of duty, or links to the past. These are sub-jectively compelling, but ask yourself if these relationships provide any benefit.

The term toxic relationship or toxic person is used in personal consultations. In general, this is a term for a person to whom we devote a lot of energy and time, but from whom we receive nothing at best or stress and negativity at worse. Toxic people may disguise themselves well as jokers and are often social and popular. The trick is that when you're with this person, you may not perceive the negative behaviors and opinions. Or maybe you do notice, but tell yourself that it's not worth spoiling a visit arguing with them. Having a toxic person in the family or as a partner makes a big difference in the long run.

What are the characteristics of toxic people and how can we learn to recognize them? Toxic people have a negative outlook and negative personalities. They see problems everywhere, and rather than looking for solutions, focus only on the problem and how it could get even worse. When one person comes up with a new idea, they immediately know that it could never work and will only make things worse. Be aware that a negative person isn't necessarily sad or depressed as it may seem. We all must forgive our friends and family from time to time and offer support. Someone with a toxic personality disguises their attitude as humor or teasing. They may say unkind things about people who aren't in the room. Someone who finds faults in friends, family, colleagues, neighbors, and partners has surely already found faults with us as well.

Toxic people can be social, assertive, and communicative. These features allow them to control conversations or social gatherings and gain attention and popularity. Although the toxicity may not be obvious at first, it can start to wear us down before we notice any dramatic changes. Our values, life goals, morals, and desire to accomplish things may begin to decline, especially if the toxic person is our partner. I have watched sadly as many talented people have abandoned their efforts for self-realization due to their partner's attitude.

Impostor Syndrome

We recently went over the difference between self-confidence and arrogance. If we want to be confident, we have to provide value and not manipulate other people to our advantage. As a result of our childhood and constantly questioning *"Am I good enough?"*, we run into a curious phenomenon that directly affects our perception of our qualifications.

This is called *impostor syndrome*[19]. It can be found in people who have all the prerequisites for confidence, but still constantly doubt themselves. The name of the phenomenon is based on the individual's perception of themselves as an imposter or fraud, who has only made it into their current position by chance and will soon be discovered by their peers as inadequate. I know plenty of people who doubt themselves like this, even though they consistently deliver above-average results. One of my clients regularly wins accolades at work, but still fears for their position and doubts their abilities.

In the previous section, we learned that self-confidence must be based in a state of self-awareness. Knowing your strengths is just as important as knowing your weaknesses and potential limits. Imposter syndrome shares one essential aspect with self-confidence – it comes from within. No one else has the power to make you confident. Good results, awards, popularity, and money will not mean much if you

---

[19] en.wikipedia.org/wiki/Impostor_syndrome
Litner J. (2020). *How to handle impostor syndrome.* Medical News Today

carry around the internal feeling of being a fraud, afraid to be found out as "not good enough". It's up to you to change your attitude.

One of the causes of impostor syndrome is a misunderstanding of the difference between arrogance and self-esteem, and fear of attracting negative attention. When we're raised our whole lives to be modest, it can be uncomfortable to be more skilled than others around us. We want to develop this and provide value and help to people, but first, we need to deal with our internal fear of being perceived as arrogant. This fear of what others think can obstruct our development. We don't want to appear too full of ourselves, so we're reluctant to talk about what we have achieved, or we minimize our success in conversations. Taking this approach only means that people won't know what we're capable of and our progress will proceed more slowly, all because we were afraid of being immodest. Being overly modest will only hurt us in the long run. One sign of the difference between self-confidence and arrogance is the willingness to accept a job at any cost—even when you know your time and your work is worth more. Turning down a promotion, new project, or contract out of modesty or self-doubt won't help others see your value.

In my own professional life, I'm constantly working on self-confidence due to my personality and my technological background, which puts a large emphasis on "room for improvement". Since I constantly see the opportunity to do things better, it's challenging to ever be satisfied or think that my work is "good enough". This feeling used to be an obstacle that made it difficult for me to get my work out in front of the right people.

If you have a similar struggle, try to focus on the work itself, rather than the results, and mentally remind yourself of your motivation.

When you're doing good work with good intentions, the results are guaranteed to come.

Imposter syndrome sounds like an unpleasant phenomenon with negative effects, however, there is something positive we can take away from it. There are two options. The first is to not let mistakes paralyze you or to use mistakes to improve and work on yourself. If you recognize imposter syndrome in yourself, do not despair. Aim to overcome it with new knowledge, so that you don't give those around you a chance to notice. Many successful people have admitted that they experienced similar feelings. A successful person is one who dispels these feelings and overcomes them with work. The second option is to close yourself off and not take risks. In this case, no results can be expected.

Pretense And Marketing Fiction

Social networks and virtual profiles allow us to present ourselves any way we want to. It's not uncommon to create 2 or 3 different internet identities. While it isn't simple to maintain such a multidimensional online life, there are still people who do it.

When we begin to doubt ourselves or feel Imposter Syndrome coming on, it isn't uncommon to turn to social media and take refuge in a successful internet identity, such as a LinkedIn profile. Exaggerations and false work experiences may appear impressive at first glance, but it's only a matter of time before we embarrass ourselves in front of real people at a meeting with clients or an interview with a potential employer.

Example: A young man wrote to me complaining that even though he reads about the shortage of IT workers, he hasn't been able to find work. He came across as arrogant, making dismissive statements such as, *"everyone except for me barely works"*, *"no one even tries to do the job well"*, *"people don't like me only because they don't like to hear criticism"*, and so on. It was clear to me why he had trouble making contacts, and it wasn't a problem with the clients.

This is only one part of the story – the hidden part. I had the opportunity to see this young man appear in public. Again, he came across as quite arrogant and commented on how others are unable to properly do their work. In public, however, he talks about how well he is doing, how many clients are interested in him, and how he has no issues finding work. When I watched his public statements, I couldn't believe my eyes. He presents himself as a confident, successful person who is in a position to evaluate and criticize the work of others. In our private correspondence, however, he was a desperate man, unable to secure contacts and feeling like the world was against him since he is so great and the rest of us so incompetent.

Be cautious any time someone presents their success story without details of failure and embarrassment along the way. These unbelievably one-directional success stories are almost always shams. One idea I like regarding career-building is as follows:

The difference between a successful and an unsuccessful person is that a successful person has failed more times than the unsuccessful one has even tried.

People who have achieved important positions and built large companies can talk at length about their stumbles. They see them as lessons in their development. Motivational lectures and positive thinking are nice, but the reality is rough. From the beginning, the dream career isn't a straight, comfortable path, but a winding road full of pitfalls and disappointments.

I recommend presenting your previous career candidly, with full acceptance of the positive and negatives, the coincidences that helped you on your way, and the lessons you learned from missteps and failures. People who present their unchallenged success and social status often do so to hide private insecurity, unhappiness, or bankruptcy. In my practice, I have begun to pick up the differences in what people do and what they say. Pay attention if you start to notice inconsistencies. The reality may be wildly different than the story they are telling. Above all, don't get caught up in comparing yourself to others. Everyone has different goals, values, visions, and priorities. The right path is not the same for everyone.

Learned Helplessness

Learned helplessness is an interesting psychological phenomenon that we can easily see in people around us. Psychologist Martin E. P. Seligman experimented with animals and noticed that when a dog couldn't control a negative stimulus (electric shock), it would fall into a state of disinterest and apathy. Later, when the animal is given the opportunity to stop the electric shocks, it will not even try to do so.

People behave in the same way. They have the opportunity to make a life change, but they lack the motivation and energy to make it happen. They're so used to problems, frustrations, or even physical pain that they're remiss to take a step towards resolving their problems. Even when provided with a solution, they may ignore or decline it.

It's surprisingly easy to fall into a state of helplessness and frustration and lose the desire to even find a solution. Depression can develop, and the brain suffering from chemical imbalance can make it almost impossible to make a change without external help.

The reason for bringing up the phenomenon of learned helplessness is that it's closely related to personal marketing and self-esteem. The process of bankruptcy begins imperceptibly. For example, if we aren't satisfied with our job, we go to work with reluctance. At the start, the situation isn't so serious that intervention is necessary. Then, burnout, disinterest, and reluctance to get out of bed and perform work duties set in. We begin to get sick more often, feel exhausted, and doctors have no physiological cause to point to. Falling into an occasional slump may not be harmful, but we must be able to get out of it ourselves within a few days.

Losing enthusiasm for work usually arises when we have no connection to our work and don't particularly enjoy it. Maybe we expected more money or a better work environment, or changes in management are causing additional stress. We feel like we're just going through the motions at work, but we're reluctant to change because we have a mortgage, a family to support, or some other reason to not want to take risks. This strained emotional state only gets worse as it goes on. It's best to pay attention to negative emotions and try to find a way to improve the situation as soon as possible. Leaving the situation alone for too long will only make fixing it more difficult in the long run.

Learned helplessness can occur in our employees, and can manifest in a drop in creativity or reliability. These employees may only do the bare minimum and cause more work for their colleagues. One person with a sufficiently negative outlook can bring down a whole team. It's important to deal with these issues with your employees and protect the company culture and atmosphere. Loss of trust in the company is a problem that is often only solved by replacing a substantial number of employees and trying to not make the same mistakes.

As marketers, we mainly deal with marketing services – how to create a more inviting website, for example. These practical tasks are at the forefront of everything that needs to be done in marketing. However, after consulting with our client, we may run into more abstract problems than just managing marketing channels. Clients often don't know how to stand apart from their competition. While our job should be to advise them on how to present what sets them and their company apart, the client may not have any idea what exactly that thing is.

Anyone can make a list of what they do, but only a select few can go beyond and describe how and why their services differ. Steve Jobs was exceptional at this. He would glaze over the technology and focus on what it did for his clients. While other manufacturers offered an mp3 player, Apple sold *"1,000 songs in your pocket"*.

Many entrepreneurs fail to present themselves as well as they could because they underestimate themselves or accumulate frustration from past failures. Learned helplessness in various forms can cause this. Opinions such as, *"I have never been good in this area"*, or *"I will never learn business"*, or "computers are complicated", or *"marketing has never worked for me"* are all forms of learned helplessness in action.

As marketers, we should consider the human side of business and company management. Otherwise, any strategy will be commercially ineffective, even if it's technically perfect from a pure marketing point of view. Revealing the motivation of individuals gives us a powerful weapon for creating a unique and significant marketing campaign that stands out from the competition.

Marketing seems to be particularly technical these days. Everywhere we see statistics, graphs, analysis, all sorts of tools, editors, online strategies, and the like. But the essence of marketing isn't in technology but in thinking! Technology is a tool and a helper. It will increase the efficiency of our activities when we know what we're doing and how to use it. With marketing principles, it doesn't matter whether you want to sell a newspaper on a city street, or if you want to design a Facebook ad campaign. Knowing and understanding these principles with help you create a successful strategy regardless of context.

Personal Marketing And
How to Perceive Reality

We've already looked at several aspects of the human mind. We will describe these in more detail through NLP (neuro-linguistic programming)[20]. Our senses are limited in their capacity to perceive different things at the same time. We can only process so many stimuli at once, and everything else is lost on our brain. Our brain does two basic tasks: It takes in information from the senses, simplifies it, and makes generalizations. For example, the amount of visual information we take in is enormous, more than our brain can process for us. This is one reason why people focus on and see different things, even when observing the same scene. Reality is a relatively vague term. Scientists may use mathematical models to define reality and predict future outcomes based on certain parameters. This allows different scientists to see and

---

[20] NLP – Neuro-linguistic programming

discuss one reality. In everyday life, it's not so simple since we deal with many subjective factors.

How can we resolve a conflict between two people when each person is talking about something different? The first step is to agree on the criteria according to which we will assess the situation. Then we should also set values and priorities to serve as benchmarks for agreement. I will give an example of one such criterion. We consider feelings important. Therefore, a benchmark of evaluation is, *"This is how I feel when..."*. This approach has proven very successful for me in resolving conflicts between analytical and emotional personality types. An analytical person doesn't take feelings into account, and it's very hard for them to grasp how important feelings might be to somebody else. The first step is to recognize that feelings matter. Ignoring this truth will only lead to further disputes. Now that the criterion is defined, we can resolve some disputes.

An example of wine tasting from the chapter Predictably Irrational demonstrates how the perception of reality is relative and fundamentally influenced by our assumptions. Let us keep in mind the following cycle, where misunderstandings can occur at every step:

- What I have to say

- How I communicate it

- How the other person understands it

- How the other person reacts based on their understanding

- How I interpret the other person's response

We see that communication is a rather complex process. Or expressed differently – we can assign communication only to points 2 and 3. All the points together then create an understanding – and that's the goal in personal relationships and marketing. The aim of the entrepreneur is not only to communicate information but to get the specific desired reaction from the communication, i.e. the customer buying the product and recommending it further.

Reality is a relative term for people. If we want to succeed in marketing by guiding and influencing people, we have to always keep this in mind. We have to ask how our potential clients see our business. When customer feedback doesn't align with our intention, we need to find a way to close the gap. We may have to change our business model or focus on another target group.

Example. Imagine that you open a restaurant and fill it with paintings that you love and bring you fond memories. You may look at them with appreciation, but perhaps the guests look at them and feel uncomfortable and decide they don't want to come back to your restaurant. It's the same set of paintings, but they elicit different emotions in different people.

Proactive Versus Reactive

The terms **proactive** and **reactive** are used a lot in business coaching. They're also significant in terms of personal marketing and decision-making. Let's take a closer look.

Reactive

A reactive approach is one which responds to a state of reality. We perceive facts and make decisions according to our perceptions. There are plenty of examples of this: The competition added cameras to phones, so now we will do that too; I got fired from my job, so now I will look for something new; I don't have a job, so I will go for training in a certain field; our sales are slipping, so we need to figure out a new approach.

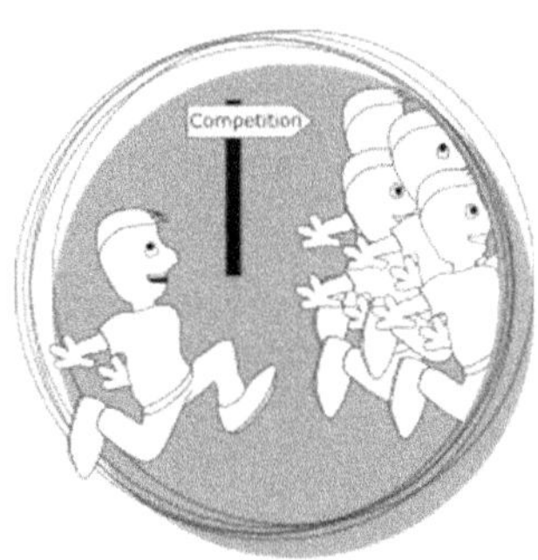

Being reactive comes naturally to us for a couple of reasons. We have clear input information–something happened and now we will respond to it. We can look for solutions that have already been used by someone else. We have a clear idea of what we want to do. We have a strong incentive to eliminate problems.

What are the disadvantages of the reactive approach? Whether in everyday life or at work, reactivity almost always means "putting out fires". This can put us into a victim mindset, which is never a good state. We may start to feel like bad things always happen to us and we're drowning in problems. We're victims of uncontrollable circumstances.

The constant feeling of having to put out fires will lead to frustration. We may start to feel like nothing is going right and our problems are only growing. This will continue until we stop what we are doing and make a drastic change: quitting our job, closing our company, leaving the country, divorcing our partner, firing employees, etc. But if we don't understand this stems from our reactive way of thinking, we will soon find ourselves in a new place with surprisingly similar problems. The cycle repeats itself.

Modern society and the fast pace of life drive more and more people into a spiral of reactive thinking. Psychologists, lifestyle coaches, and even fortune tellers find they have more work than ever. Many people feel faced with more problems than they can handle on their own. But there is good news! Our attitudes and ways of thinking depend on us. They are changeable!

Proactive

A **proactive** approach to life means **looking ahead, dreaming, having big goals, and planning.** Vision and dreaming alone are not enough. Proactivity is inextricably linked to endurance, determination, and self-development. We must be open to mistakes and embarrassments that are guaranteed to await us. Thinking about the future and creating a plan is extremely important because it allows us to prepare for different scenarios that can happen. Even still, you can't be prepared for everything. Preparedness and willingness to adapt mark the difference between failure and success.

I have already mentioned that reactivity comes more naturally to us. However difficult the situation, we face it from within the bounds of our comfort zone. A proactive approach, on the other hand, requires more effort, more creativity, and a willingness to try things a different way and leave the comfort zone to face new challenges. This approach is more challenging, and many people simply aren't interested in doing things proactively. They have a comfortable alternative – to get carried off by the current of their problems and vent their frustration over a beer to their friends. All this without the slightest input of energy towards change. By resigning to life's circumstances in this way, they can expect disappointment, jealousy, and suspicion of others who don't seem to suffer as they do.

Example. We can observe reactivity even in major corporations. In the year 2000, Yahoo was the #1 search engine with over 50% of the market share and millions in profits. One big competitor was Altavista, another search engine. The companies watched each other closely and even copied each other's strategies. They both wanted their opponent under control. Watching is always reactive because it takes time to innovate. What happened to Yahoo? It was completely outcompeted by a start-up created by two students – Google. Google revolutionized the search algorithm and overall site ranking. Within a few years, 90% of internet searches ran through Google.

It wasn't Yahoo's existing competitors that outcompeted it, but rather a completely unknown company with a novel approach.

There are several similar examples: Facebook overtook Friendster and Myspace. Apple and Nokia competed for the mobile phone market until Samsung surpassed them both. Nokia previously occupied almost half of the global mobile phone market, but even global influence and a massive budget for development and market couldn't protect it from collapsing. No budget can compensate for poor decisions in marketing and technology.

How to Replace Reactivity
With Proactivity?

The first step in proactive thinking is to admit that our challenges and mistakes help us to develop. A large part of learning to walk is just falling down a lot. It can't be any other way. The brain needs to learn not only how to communicate with our feet and tell them which way to go, but also what happens when our body falls. Setbacks, mistakes, and constant tests of our abilities are all part of making progress. That much is clear. The trouble is that from early childhood, parents raise us to fear mistakes. Schools only continue this bad habit by assigning our mistakes lower marks, regardless of whether or how those mistakes may have enhanced our learning experience. The idea that mistakes should be avoided at all costs is one we carry with us. The consequence of this is that many people don't like to try new things, and prefer to stay in their comfort zone, regardless of the consequences. The consequences are objective and rational. The comfort zone is all about feeling and perception. It's clear to see that many people prefer the security of their comfort zone, despite the objectively obvious negative consequences: earning less money, not having any training or job prospects, being unable to find a partner, or find the motivation to take care of their health. The sense of comfort prevails over the desire for change because people are afraid to make mistakes.

The second step in taking a proactive approach is to focus on what you want. Ideally, write everything down. If you don't like doing this sort of thing by yourself, ask a friend, partner, or coach to do it with you. The goal is to write down everything you want to achieve without worrying about limits or external constraints. I recommend creating your list practically and pragmatically, focusing on what you want and not your wildest fantasies. Otherwise, you step into the realm of esoteric and blind faith in success.

In the previous section, I wrote about the difference between self-esteem and arrogance. Now it's time to put this knowledge to work. When creating your list of "*What I want*", be sure to focus on self-confidence and providing value. Of course, you could put things on your list like millions in a bank account, a yacht, a big house, and an expensive car. But that's an arrogant approach. How are you going to get these things? Someone will just give them to you?

Your "*What I want*" list should be about providing value to the world. For example, "*I want to be a singer and create great performances for my fans*"; "*I want to have an IT business and develop mobile apps that will help users succeed*"; "*I want to be a respected doctor and engage in research that will result in a better understanding of how to cure the body of disease*"; "*I want to be a racecar driver to entertain people and push the limits of motorsports*"; "*I want to grow organic fruit to help people eat healthier and live longer*".

Whatever appears on your list should express the transfer of value from you to your customers/audience/patients. Self-esteem is applied here by focusing on our strengths and activities that we enjoy and fulfill us. Successful people find passion and enjoyment in what they do. They see their work as their mission. It doesn't matter what anyone else's opinion of their idea was – they were determined, kept trying, and eventually succeeded. This is true of Edison and his inventions, the Wright brothers and their airplane, Pasteur and his new pharmaceuticals, Fleming and the discovery of penicillin, and many others like them.

The third step in proactive thinking is to consider what options you have at your disposal to help you achieve what you wrote down in step two. You now have your vision of where you are going or where you want to be in the future, but how will you get there? Now think about your current situation: emotionally, financially, physically, and according to your family or educational status. The more areas you consider in this step, the better mental picture you will have of your situation and your available resources.

Of all the options at your disposal, chose a few that will best help you embark on the path you have envisioned. If you don't pick it right the first time, it doesn't matter! Mistakes still provide valuable information that will help the process. Think ahead of what the journey will look like. Look for inspiration in books or on the internet, and read the stories of others who have achieved similar goals. You don't have to spend years studying, but it's a good idea to gather as much information as possible and prepare for possible scenarios.

The fourth step on the road to proactivity is to get up and start working. You have written down your vision, described your current situation, considered all possible options, and prepared for various scenarios. Now it's time to get to work in the real world. Do you want to start a business? Go out and apply for a business license.

If you can't leave your work due to a mortgage, then you will have to takes these steps during your spare time. Financial security is not achieved on the first day. You still need to deal with your current situation to get where you want to be. Saying that it's impossible is just an excuse. Your attitude has to be *"How can I make this possible?"*

The fifth step will be "stepping" out of your comfort zone. This phrase is often used, although many don't know exactly what it means. It simply means that we should commit to doing activities that we aren't necessarily good at right now and may not even enjoy doing. If we want to succeed in business, we must present ourselves in front of strangers. Yes, the first few meetings will be unpleasant, perhaps you will do something embarrassing. Don't worry about it! It's necessary that you learn, and mistakes are part of that. Thinking *"I am afraid I won't succeed"* is a very effective way to kill your progress and motivation. Fear will only lead us back to the comfort zone and our brain will rationalize that we never wanted to make a change in the first place. Typical examples of this type of backward rationalization are

"*Running a business just isn't for me*"; "*I don't enjoy it as much as I thought I would*"; "someone has to do my job, and we can't all become rich". Our brains will do this automatically without our conscious input. It's for this very reason that we must claw our way out of our comfort zone and into the unknown world of situations, even though it will feel unpleasant and intimidating in the beginning.

Why go through all of this? Because the result is getting to live a happy and fulfilled life with a job that we enjoy. Yes, the brain may comfort us and rationalize our decisions and give us all sorts of arguments as to why we don't want to take a step towards improvement. But this feeling subsides and will only be replaced with: "*Oh the neighbor is doing very well. They have another new car in the driveway, while I'm stuck in my boring job, waiting for the weekend to come*". The cycle of frustration and discontent continues.

Keep in mind that success is more than money and expensive cars. In many cases, the value may not be externally visible, for example traveling, donating to charities, helping children, going to exclusive events, and so on. Money is important, but once you make enough to cover expenses, money ceases to be a major motivating factor. As we move up Maslow's Pyramid, we're interested in more abstract values and we have higher goals.

The sixth step of developing proactive thinking is to go back to the beginning, repeat and improve in the process. Step five is about real events and work. Now what is important is that you don't get devoured by the work. Always keep your vision of the future in mind. This is the only way to be able to create and influence your surroundings to achieve your goal. Everything that humans have come up with started as just an idea in someone's head. An abstract concept. Nothing more than a vision. Then the vision was translated into work and a real-world result was created. That is proactive thinking.

We can't allow ourselves to forget about the work that our mind is doing by dreaming and creating a vision. It may not sound pragmatic, but this mental exercise will reinforce your determination and drive to keep working. Your initial stroke of inspiration will not last forever, so you must renew it from new sources. We, as humans, are changing and the world is evolving around us – faster today than ever before. To see new opportunities, we need to find the time. First, to perceive them, and second, to think about and discuss them. When we drive forward with our heads down, we will miss a lot of interesting opportunities around us.

The power of the marketing mindset is the focus on something deeper – whether it be our clients, employees, or the market as a whole. Commonly, new clients will come to business meetings with the expectation that I can create some marketing campaign for them that will miraculously elevate their business. Of course, there is no such campaign, and even the client knows this deep down. After a more detailed discussion, we will get down to the deeper factors influencing the company, such as micro-management, dissatisfaction, and burnout. Often, small business owners will find that they are missing a key component for success. Usually, this starts with initial success and the business growing bigger. The owner may begin to feel in over their head and unsure of what to do next. This overworked and unfulfilled feeling can translate into a reactive approach to problem-solving. New business owners find that their role is constantly changing, and they have to adapt to new tasks which are unfamiliar and difficult. In the chapter about marketing processes, we use the example of a hair-dresser. I always bring a similar document with me to business meetings. My answer is that the client doesn't yet need online marketing, they need to build a systematic concept, and then effective marketing will emerge out of it.

The Proactive Versus Reactive Approach in Marketing

As we explained in previous chapters, proactivity means thinking ahead, preparing for possible scenarios, and actively creating our circumstances. Reactivity is characterized by putting out fires and always needing to respond to external situations. In my business, the reactive approach is manifested in one sentence, which is a starting point for many of my projects:

"Why don't clients go to my website and buy my products?"

The vast majority of entrepreneurs who are not doing well ask this question. What is wrong with this question? There is no satisfactory answer! Negatively framed questions don't bring positive answers. They only bring the focus to problems and mistakes, rather than to solutions and how to enact them proactively. Let's swap out this negatively framed question for a positively framed one.

"I want to figure out how to draw clients into my store to buy my products."

A positively framed inquiry encourages a constructive, solutions-based answer. We won't spend our time thinking about what we didn't do right before. We are focused on the current moment and how to improve the state of things here and now.

♦ Do I know what the client is buying from me? (The value, not the product itself.)

♦ Are my products of sufficient quality?

♦ Am I providing a solution to a target market that needs it?

♦ Are potential customers aware of the value I provide?

♦ Do people have a reason to care about me and my company?

♦ Do I offer more than my competition?

♦ Can I meet the requirements of my clients?

These are examples of useful questions with straightforward answers that you can use to drive your business forward. Sometimes, it happens that we make mistakes in our assumptions and end up not getting the results we expected. It's not a big deal, especially as you're still learning and developing. In the process of creating, mistakes are inevitable, but you can learn to take them positively. Say to yourself: *"I have done the best that I can at this point. I'm always improving, and the next steps will be even better."*

Internal And External Motivation

The concepts of motivation, inspiration, stimulation, and manipulation are extremely abstract, and their understanding varies across people and languages. In HR and leadership contexts, the concept of motivation is mostly thought of in the external sense – salary, benefits, team building, time-off and so on. Companies are looking for ways to externally motivate their employees. This chapter aims to emphasize the importance of internal motivation and how it can inspire people.

In different languages, the words *"motivation"* and *"inspiration"* are used differently[21]. In the English language, motivation is generally used in an external context, while inspiration is used as internal. In some other languages, inspiration is less commonly used: in place of *"inner inspiration"*, some languages commonly refer to *"inner motivation"*[22].

---

[21] www.etymonline.com/index.php?term=inspiration
[22] Kopřiva P. et all. (2012). *Respect and be respected.*

The word inspiration comes from Latin, and its usage and meaning have changed throughout society. Seven centuries ago, the expression of inspiration was used in religious texts with the meaning of *"direct divine intervention"* or *"direct influence of God"*. The prefix "in" in the word indicates the inside or the direction inwards. Later, the word was adopted by the French in the form of *"inspiracion"*, in the sense of inhalation of thought. In Old English, we also find the meaning as *"breathing life into the body"*. In more modern Latin, we find it in the form *"inspiratio,"*, which, once again, has the prefix *"in"*, meaning from within, and the root of the word *"spirare"*, meaning to breathe-in. It's also used in connection to *"spirit"*, emphasizing its esoteric importance for the soul/spirit. Inspiration, in short, means to take in energy and meaning.

The word **motivation** takes its meaning from the Latin *"movere"*, which means to move or agitate[23]. You can see that the words motivation and inspiration fit together nicely. Inspiration comes from within; it's the idea or vision of achieving something. It can be *"inhaled"* from some inspirational surroundings, or purely come into being on its own. The motivation is then about realizing these visions and *moving* towards the goal. Let's look at both expressions in further detail.

External motivation

Social networks are filled with motivational quotes designed to inspire us and awaken our desire for achievement. The question is whether

---

[23] enhancedmotivation.com/movere

external motivation can truly inspire someone in the first place. Companies attempt to externally motivate employees, and parents do the same with their children. Does external motivation even work?

The basis of external motivation is an incentive to take action from our surroundings. Something motivates us to do or not do a certain activity. Good grades are often motivated by parental praise or incentives. Compliance with the law is motivated by a desire to avoid high penalties for violations. Employees are motivated by the potential for higher wages, or the fear of unemployment.

The trouble with external motivation is that it only works in the short term. Praise wears off, rewards stop being exciting, and small salary increases don't make up for the feeling of performing unnecessary and monotonous work. As the effects of external motivation wear off, some managers turn to manipulation, but even manipulation has a short self-life and is more taxing than external motivation. The *"carrot and stick"* method, or just the *"stick"* method, have been tested by many parents and employers, and in the end, they usually wind up with exactly the opposite results of what they had hoped for.

Example. The American car manufacturer GM has been testing various methods to increase its sales since the 1990s. One such attempt was using a financial incentive, *"cashback"*, to encourage people to buy new cars. The customer received several hundred dollars back after purchasing a new car. People got used to not paying the sticker price, but this strategy deprived GM of profit, so they eventually had to stop the campaign. Customers accustomed to the discounts lost interest in GM cars and turned to Japanese manufacturers instead. It was a disaster for GM. Financial external motivation only caused problems in the long run.

If external motivation fades with time, how can we improve upon it? How can we maintain the effects of motivation in the long term? The answer is **internal motivation** and **inspiration**.

Internal motivation

Internal motivation comes from our personal belief that the work we do has a purpose and brings us joy. Our drive comes from the desire for knowledge, success, or recognition. It's not so much about money. Even when someone tells you that they want to earn money, it's usually to get something else which can be exchanged for money: education, travel, adrenaline, security, etc.

Internal motivation is very high on Maslow's pyramid. Once we can cover our basic needs, such as housing, food, and healthcare, then our focus will shift to more abstract needs. Recognition is one of the most common. And since our goal is abstract at this point, we must think abstractly about how to get there. This may seem vaguely esoteric at first glance. Even if what we want is realistic and grounded, it still helps to see ourselves from a higher angle. Great results are not achieved by figuring out how to better tidy up your office or save 1% on gasoline. Success is achieved by focusing on more abstract concepts, such as our inner goals. What will make us happy, not just in the moment, but long-term? Happiness means that everyday work brings joy and a sense of fulfillment. We're doing something that makes sense. That's exactly what inner motivation is.

The cornerstones of internal motivation are:

- Meaningful day-to-day activities

- Possibilities and freedom to make decisions

- Feedback and self-development

- Fulfillment of internal needs and values

For many people, they struggle to find motivation within themselves, as past frustration or failures keep them from dreaming big or having ambitious goals. They become so resigned that any large goal feels unrealistic. If you feel this sense of resignation personally, it may be time to seek encouragement from a coach or personal development specialist. It's a worthwhile investment!

Motivation And Inspiration
Within a Company

It's easier to find our motivation than it is to ignite it in other people. To discover the internal engine of another, it's necessary to get to know them better first. If we oversee a team of people, whether as a manager or a business owner, our task is to understand and develop the individual motivations of our employees. The vast majority of executives don't even attempt this and have nothing to motivate their employees, except the *"carrot and stick"* approach of external motivation. This isn't the best approach since external motivations only work in the short term and aren't conducive to interpersonal relations.

An employee can start with their own internal motivation, do good work that they find fulfilling, and have their motivation spoiled by the company they work for. This is the consequence of poor management. As a rule, frustrated employees will leave. It isn't necessarily the work, but the senseless systems, overloaded bureaucracy, and incompetent direct superiors that cause employees to reach a breaking point. According to one Gallup[24] poll, as many as 50% of employees cited their direct supervisors as the main reason they decided to seek new employment. In at least half of the statements, the employees

---

[24] fortune.com/2015/04/02/quit-reasons/

didn't leave work because of the company as such, but as a means to escape bad management.

Finding and engaging the internal motivation of employees is an essential role for good management. Unfortunately, this role is largely ignored. New managers don't know how to inspire and ignite the internal motivation of their employees, even if they already suspect that external motivation isn't a long-term solution. So how to proceed? The most important factor for inspiring others is knowing your motivation and being able to present your passion. There isn't much to it. When we work in a field that excites and fulfills us, we radiate more enthusiasm. When our enthusiasm is apparent and radiates out, it can serve as a source of inspiration for others.

Why do companies need inspiration? It's incredibly difficult to lead people to do a good job at work if they don't believe in their job or are bored with what they're doing. A successful company is one that can inspire employees. This will allow them to develop and maintain their internal motivation. This idea can be summed up in a well-known statement:

"It doesn't make sense to hire smart people and tell them what to do; we hire smart people so they can tell us what to do."

Steve Jobs

Self-driven people are both creative and responsible. They work to improve themselves and do better work for clients. It's not necessary to constantly monitor them and look for ways to motivate them externally. They do good work because that's what they want for themselves. The work provides them with the fulfillment that supports their continued enthusiasm and drive. They make a good name for the company and share in its success. This type of employee is highly valuable, and the company should take care that their motivation isn't stifled.

How can we inspire others? Many books have been written on this topic. Every author or famous personality has their take. Some methods can be easily adapted, others not so much. There is always a common factor where inspiration if only theoretically, can work. The essential basis for inspiring others is to genuinely be passionate about what you do and enjoy doing it. If we can stir up inspiration in others, we can positively influence them – but the feelings alone won't be enough. It's necessary to connect specific people with work that aligns with their passions and interests. If we try to inspire athletes to get involved in selling technology, the results probably won't be great, regardless of our passion for the subject. The inspiration only works if it's related to the personal interests of those we are trying to inspire. If we can meet this condition, our results can exceed expectations.

Keep in mind that factual knowledge alone doesn't lead to success. For a better understanding of the connection, we briefly turn to the human brain. Overall, the brain doesn't respond much to hard data. The neocortex is the area of the brain responsible for much of what we consider to be human intelligence. This area shows the greatest difference from our ape cousins. There is trouble here in the formation of communication channels. The neocortex perceives information from lower parts of the brain well – we know when we're coughing or sneezing, experiencing a fever, and so on. Unfortunately, lower sections of the brain ignore the neocortex and its "will". We can't stop sneezing and coughing, we don't consciously affect our heart rate, and we practically can't help feeling scared.

The neocortex perceives situations in other parts of the brain and body immediately, however, it can't effectively influence the lower, more evolutionarily basal parts of the brain. For example, the first time we get on a rollercoaster, we feel some fear and adrenaline; our stomach clenches, our pulse races, and we unconsciously hold the safety rail more tightly. The brain is sensing danger. At this moment, rational thought is pushed aside. Saying *"don't worry, just enjoy it"* to the brain isn't going to have much effect. By the second, third, or fourth time we ride a rollercoaster, the brain settles down and stops reacting to the initially perceived danger. We can finally peacefully enjoy the ride without white-knuckling the safety rail for dear life.

Let's take a quick look at the brain to see how communication between rational thoughts and irrational emotions influence our behavior. As rational as we want to be, we are limited by our evolutionary biology, which has supplied us with a gap between what we know we should do and how we act in reality. The same goes for inspiration.

Telling school children to work hard and keep studying because it will give them more opportunities later in life doesn't do much to inspire them. Similarly, saying *"I need to lose weight to fit into my favorite dress"* doesn't work. Human emotions generally ignore these rational suggestions in the neocortex. Before we can effectively lose weight, build a business, or quit smoking, our emotions will continually remind us how much we love food, being lazy, and having a cigarette in hand. Since the neocortex immediately gets logical information about how we should behave to achieve our goal, it immediately triggers a wave of rationalizations for why we should just carry on the way we always have. *"Even if I slim down enough to fit into that dress again, I have nowhere to wear it"*, or *"I can just buy a new dress"*, or *"I don't smoke that much, it isn't so bad"*. Each of us has examples from our own lives. The emotional inertia wins out and our resigned neocortex makes rationalizations to defend our inaction.

If you want to effectively inspire others, make a point of learning how they feel now versus how they want to feel. Only then can you propose a way to work towards their desired state. Of course, to achieve a goal, some certain steps or actions must be taken, but it's up to the individual to find their way. Inspiration isn't handing someone a step-by-step manual on how to achieve a goal. No one likes being told what to do. Effective inspiration should be a wake-up call to start working hard to improve one's business, health, or life.

There are numerous how-to manuals for losing weight, healthy eating, quitting smoking, or starting a business. They fail mostly because people don't want to take the first step. It isn't a lack of information; we all know that smoking or not exercising is bad for us. Our neocortex knows this too. What about our emotional system, which should spring us into action? No dice. Smoking or extra weight is brushed off because of the positive emotions associated with cigarettes and food. Those positive associations are enough to lull our emotional systems into complacency. The brain says to us: *"the opinion of the neocortex doesn't matter. Let's go to the fridge. There is some ice-cream we can eat and feel good."*

In my consulting practice with my clients, I emphasize the need to combine marketing with inspiration. This is the most effective form of marketing because the goal is to awaken emotions in potential clients. This always generates better results than information alone. Even on a small marketing budget, this method can lead us to new clients and help us grow. If we pass off the responsibility of marketing at the start, we lose the momentum to communicate the right feelings to our potential clients directly. The company may have trouble finding clients because the clients have no emotion to associate with the company. Marketing agencies can do a great job for larger, established companies where emotional values are already known to clients – whether they're selling cars, beer, chocolates, or perfumes. This type of marketing builds on brand history and customer experience.

For a new company or new product, we need to emphasize abstract values in the form of inspiration. We can do this easily if we're passionate about our work. Customers will be attracted to our business because of our enthusiasm. If they fall in love with the product too, they will become repeat customers and recommend us further. When people know what emotion they're getting when they shop with us, then we can introduce them to news, discounts, new products, and events. The goal at this level of marketing is to get potential customers interested enough to care about new products or offerings.

However, if someone else takes on the marketing and presentation of the company at the start, they won't be able to provide the same value as the company founder. Marketing itself will become less efficient and much more expensive. The advertising campaigns typically designed by ad agencies are known for using the "proven" 4P model.

If you run a small company or manage your own business, try to inspire, and focus on the emotions of your clients. How do clients feel now and what can your product do to improve their state of being? If you've recognized that your marketing is too embedded in the 4P model, work on transitioning to the SIVA model. Make a point of presenting yourself, your story, and the value you provide. Getting personal is a strong marketing strategy.

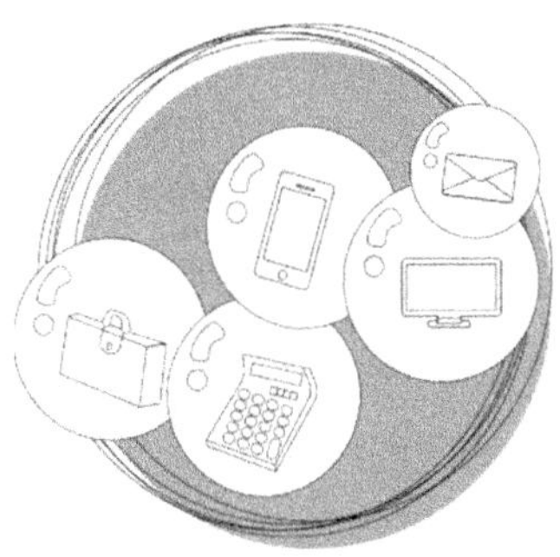

Starting a Business After A Successful Career in Corporate? Watch Out for New Roles!

Many new companies are started by people who have built a successful career in the corporate sphere. They start to feel that corporations are holding them back, and there's no reason they can't do the same thing on their own in a company where they get to be the boss...

Although the experience of working in a corporate environment is valuable, it isn't easy to see the business comprehensively from the vantage point of an employee. Even after 10 years at one company, there will still be aspects of the business employees don't fully understand. An employee may get the feeling that the owner is taking advantage of them and leave the company to start a similar business under their guidance. This is how a lot of unsuccessful projects start out. Why? Because the new business is standing on a weak foundation, regardless of the success the new business owner had in their previous position.

Example. My client built a very successful career as a recruitment manager in a medium-sized company. She oversaw recruiting, training, and managing new people. She helped push the company forward and was extremely well paid. When she decided to leave to start her own business, management was working very hard to hold on to her.

This client started her own company with the same focus she had in her former position. The first issue we had to deal with was personal marketing. Because she already had a good career in corporate, she wanted to protect her identity from any potential business failure. She decided it was best to defend herself by never publishing her name or photographs of herself. She wanted to put a lot of energy into building a brand but had only a low budget for advertising.

Tip: Regarding the name of your new company – nobody cares. The only success we can bring to the company is in finding people with experience, a good attitude, and the ability to solve problems. Even our clients don't have any personal interest in us yet. They only want to know what we can bring them. Our name, history, and a previous career in corporate aren't at all interesting if the client doesn't know what we can do for them. See phases 1 and 2 of the chapter on the purchasing process.

My client soon came across the reality of the situation. Outside the corporate world, her name didn't interest anyone and it wasn't bringing in any business on its own. This can hurt the psyche of a person. Everything she thought was worthy of admiration suddenly meant nothing. This realization can come with a sense of confusion and despair. After many years of success that now nobody cared about, what is a person to do?

Just because a successful career isn't interesting in the first phase of building a business doesn't mean that experience wasn't valuable. Quite the opposite. It can prove an asset, if only later on in the process – once we gain confidence and a little business traffic. How to sell your knowledge – this is the task of the marketing mindset. The answer is to focus on the client and what they care about, not on ourselves and our past.

Tip. If there is a large marketing budget for the brand, personal marketing can be in the background. However, this brand-based approach requires the brand name to be everywhere in the eyes of potential clients. This means television ads, radio spots, internet marketing. It takes a lot! A marketing budget of a few hundred dollars won't cut it.

A New Role

In the chapter on marketing processes, we described the role of entrepreneur, technician, and manager. These roles all have to be fulfilled for the company to function properly. In the corporate sphere, jobs are built around narrow sets of tasks and responsibilities. Corporations can't afford to let all their know-how fall on the shoulders of just one or a few individuals. For years, corporate employees have become more specialized and focused on their responsibilities.

On the other hand, when one person begins to build a company, they become responsible for everything. They may find themselves faced with tasks they didn't even know existed. Every task not done stays unfinished. There is nowhere to hide or shrug off responsibility on others. This means closing deals, making contracts, marketing, managing personnel, accounting, and even cleaning and inventory. It's necessary to have at least a basic overview of everything, even if employees are hired to work in that area. The responsibility and range of new obligations are two factors that often deter prospective entrepreneurs. Staying in a corporate environment and building a career in the safety of a large company has some undeniable appeal.

The second essential element of the new company is the fact that it has no history. The market isn't aware of our brand and probably doesn't know us either. All we have is the ability to solve a specific type of problem. Large companies get orders in a different way than small ones. It's essential for new business owners to quickly adapt to their role and do it well. The success of the company and its future depends on it.

When you start out working for yourself, you may be overwhelmed by the number of tasks you have to take care of, many of which are completely new to you. Marketing, web management, technology, CRM, business, accounting and taxes, legal obligations, security, recruitment, and so on. Have no fear! A business mentor can help you get started with these tasks. It's invaluable to be guided in the early steps by someone who knows what to do, and that you take on new tasks one at a time. As we become more confident, we can take on more. Having a business mentor will help you to progress more quickly and with fewer setbacks.

Handling New Tasks

When you apply for a contract or a new position at work, the person in charge of the selection process will take into account your previous experience. This can cause problems in today's fast-pasted society. It's often essential that you learn new concepts or know how to use new technology or software. The world has never changed as rapidly as it does today. This trend of acceleration will only continue.

Today, when someone proudly says: *"I understand this well; I have been doing it for 20 years"*, it doesn't carry the same prestige. That statement mainly implies, *"For 20 years I haven't extended my boundaries or learned anything new."*

When presenting ourselves, we may feel the need to overdo our own experience or to invent it directly to get a contract for which we don't have enough experience.

Years ago, when I oversaw fifth-year students' exercises as a PhD student, I maintained the utmost sincerity about my knowledge. There was only a small age gap between me and the students, and the danger that someone might ask a question I didn't immediately have the answer to was real. I was never ashamed to answer, *"I don't know, I will find out and explain it to you next time."* Taking this approach never diminished my authority or credibility. The students even praised it in their evaluation questionnaires.

In my business practice, I regularly encounter new tasks. When a client asks me about a previous experience with the same problem, I openly tell them that I don't have extensive experience in that particular area. At the same time, I will highlight other projects or assumptions and knowledge that I see as key to a successful solution. Open access has never closed my door before, and my impression is that it's more likely to help me get business. People fail to realize how obvious it can be when they make up experience they don't have. Our partners recognize it in negotiations, causing them to automatically lose confidence in us. My advice is to just be honest because the truth will probably be evident anyway.

The more innovative our field is, the more we encounter unknown problems and situations. Just because we don't have direct experience yet doesn't mean we can't complete the task. When we find ourselves in a similar business situation, it will always be helpful to acknowledge limitations in your experience while also demonstrating other important assets. Of course, a potential customer needs a certain guarantee. It doesn't necessarily need to be a guarantee of exact knowledge of the same type of project. Reliability, a pleasant demeanor, open communication, the ability to solve problems, and a passion for the work are all other valuable qualities that help to balance a lack of exact experience for a new task.

Online Marketing

Online marketing is the most dynamic area of marketing today. Substantial changes happen several times a year, so few companies have the time and resources to monitor and apply everything to their business. Online marketing evolves so fast that the vast majority of companies are working with outdated information to inform their decisions and expectations. What worked a few weeks ago is already outdated. Or it only works under different conditions, and for a different price.

Many companies of all sizes choose to outsource their online marketing to an agency because it can be a large task. As hiring an agency to manage online marketing is usually the first choice, let's look at some of the pros and cons.

PESO – A Mix For Digital Marketing

Marketing mixes (also known as models or frameworks) help us prepare marketing strategies, divide our target audience into smaller groups, and communicate with our clients. In each category of a marketing mix, potential clients are in different phases with differing levels of expectations and commitment to purchasing. Therefore, we need to approach each group from a different marketing standpoint, with focus targeted to meet their concerns – price, value, availability, discounts, features, etc.).

While preparing a marketing strategy, look at each group individually. For example, if our client doesn't have a large budget, but can invest time and knowledge, then having the client create advertising content and share it on social media will be a better use of resources than experimenting with paid PPC advertising. On the other hand, if you work for a large client looking to achieve immediate results, then PPC advertising is a better choice.

Understanding the advantages and disadvantages of individual groups allows us to take a large complex problem (i.e. a comprehensive marketing strategy) and divide it up into more manageable tasks. This will also help us to know what skills we need in new employees or what kind of external experts we should consult with, and determine the KPI (key performance indicators) of evaluation metrics.

	Pros	Cons
Paid	Scalable, predictable, fast results	Doesn't build trust, high price, no cumulative effect
Earned	Third-party involvement helps build trust, can be very cost-effective, marketing effect can be long-lasting	Results of third-party involvement are unpredictable, doesn't scale easily, may require considerable effort
Shared	Higher level of trust, can be very cost-effective (especially if virality is achieved)	Degree of sharing or virality is hard to predict, requires significant effort to generate quality material, doesn't scale easily
Owned	Complete access to all platforms, ability to edit or remove content at will, quality content generates long-term results (cumulative effect)	Platforms alone may not generate revenue and require other marketing activities, expensive to create

Now, let's take a look at PESO. The letter **P** stands for *paid* – as in PPC ads, Facebook ads webpage banners, and so on – anything we have to pay for to get exposure for our product. The **E** stands for *earned* – when our product impresses someone enough to promote it without charging us for advertising, for example, a shout-out on a blog, radio, or television program. **S** stands for *shared* – marketing content that gets shared across social networks is extremely valuable.

High-quality popular content can go viral, achieving a level of exposure worth thousands of dollars. That is why so many marketers try to create viral content. The **O** stands for *owned* – any websites, blogs, or social media sites the company itself runs. Content created on "owned" channels have the benefit of being controllable. We can publish what is appropriate and adapt content to changing demands. The downside is that marketing on "owned" channels isn't very effective unless it gains external attention.

The previous table summarized the pros and cons of these strategies. One strategy isn't inherently better than any other. The appropriate strategy will depend on the business, their product, their marketing budget, and the target audience. Understanding these strategies will allow us to approach digital marketing from multiple angles, and benefit from it in multiple contexts.

Before Starting To Work With An Agency

Marketing agencies work by monitoring and applying new information to their campaigns as quickly as possible. It's wise to hire specialists in online marketing who know the field and how to develop a campaign within it. We shouldn't underestimate this assignment.

Before hiring a marketing agency (or even just an individual to manage social media), we have to be clear about what we want to show and why: What value we offer our clients and who exactly our clients are. We should have thought about what our budget and financial objectives are and consider our expectations. This is precisely the area that many agencies and freelancers don't give enough attention to.

Their starting position tends to be budget and goals in the form of KPI[25]. For example, if we want online advertising in the form of PPC[26], it's unlikely that they will ask us why we want it and what values we want to present. The answer *"I want to reach new clients"* is too general and will be used by everyone. The agency will then have no choice but to use the 4P model. If we have a large enough budget, its task will be to bring visitors at the lowest possible price. The bigger the budget, the more room there is for experimentation. The task of generating visits is likely to work, but there will be problems with closing deals – conversions.

The first complication we encounter is the conversion price. Currently, online marketing is quite expensive. We should consider whether visitors who have yet to buy something can be reached again and for a lower price, by phone or email for example. If we are already paying $0.50 for each visitor, we should use the system to get their contact info. To do this, we must provide something valuable in exchange. A mere *"sign up for our newsletter"* isn't enough incentive. People value their privacy and aren't looking to add to their junk mail.

Even if the vast majority don't buy something, we are paying for their visit and should try to get their information. There are many tools on the market to analyze webpage visitors. Data will always help to improve the purchasing process and the site overall. The difference between a successful and unsuccessful firm lies with the data. Large companies have the data and know-how to use it. It helps them adapt to changes and maintain their success. We should pay attention to the

---

[25] KPI – Key Performance Indicator – For example, the number of new accounts, sales, or e-book downloads.
[26] PPC – Pay Per Click – For example, Google Ads.

growing number of tools and software that we use and how much they will cost us. Despite all this, we don't necessarily have to work a lot harder to see better profits – and higher revenue isn't the same as higher profits.

The next complication when hiring an ad agency is the larger the agency, the greater the division of tasks. One person takes care of posts on your Facebook page, the next watches over the ad, and the third suggests graphics. Someone else oversees PR and your media image. This division of tasks may result in the loss of common vision and a unified approach across platforms. Each agency employee takes care of several clients and their overall marketing approach will be similar across all their clients. The effectiveness of the campaign will depend largely on the budget. If the campaign is impersonal, lacks a story or connection with a personality, it will be more costly to gain interest. This type of advertising doesn't spread by itself. As soon as we stop paying for or promoting it, the effects will be lost.

On the other hand, when we think about the vision of the project and connect it with the story and fate of people, then even marketing has a much greater impact; it can spread itself, even virally. The results of any ad campaign will be cumulative, meaning it will be responsible for current sales, but also influence sales in the next week or the following month. Even when the ad is turned off, its message will continue to spread among our clients in the form of likes, shares, and recommendations.

Before hiring a marketing agency, think about the project's vision, its story, how it connects people. Prepare answers to a few key questions:

♦ Why are we in business, and what do we offer? What is the value, not the product, that we offer, i.e. Why should people do business with us?

♦ Why should people identify with our company; what are our values?

♦ Why do we do what we do; what motivates us?

♦ How did we get to our current position; what is our story?

♦ Can we implement the SIVA model?

If we have clearly defined answers to the above questions, then the agency's work for us will be significantly more accurate, and we can easily evaluate whether the goals we set out to achieve are being met.

Another recommendation before signing on with an ad agency is to have mastery over your own operations. Product delivery should be in flawless working order, and there should be a crisis plan, ready to be implemented in case of an emergency. The performance of any marketing agency ultimately depends on the company's ability to deliver its product satisfactorily.

Summary: If you're building your own small business, it's best you view external marketers and agencies as tools. We can use them, but we're in charge of determining what they do. Whether they work efficiently and generate results depends primarily on us. A gilded hammer and chisel don't make a better statue than ordinary ones. Moreover, a hammer and chisel in unskilled hands won't do any good – they cannot carve stone by themselves. A blunt chisel, however, can ruin a whole project.

What should you take away from this analogy? We should start with ourselves and develop our own prowess. Then, it's important to choose quality tools and guide them to do what we need them to do.

Online Marketing: Not simple
And Not cheap

Many of my clients start out quite naïve about how online marketing works and how the pricing is structured. Some assume online marketing will be simple and inexpensive. Their plan is as follows – create a product or service (typically only slightly different from the competitors and without substantial added value). Invest the majority of resources into creating a webpage. Hire an ad agency to generate visits to the webpage as cheaply as possible. Sit back and watch the business grow and invest more into marketing later. The company grows without any problems.

I always start by strongly cautioning start-ups against being tempted by simple solutions. They're guaranteed to be used by someone else. The plan I just laid out is one used by many and has only a slim chance of success. The smaller the marketing budget, the greater the risk of failure.

There are several flaws in this naive business plan. Sometimes, we hear that it's not the product that's important, but the marketing. This isn't entirely true. The product and its quality are extremely important. The more competitive the field, the more important the product quality is. When there are many available alternatives, a lack of quality will not be tolerated. Quality isn't a competitive advantage; it's a base requirement.

The second flaw, and the theme of this chapter, is the assumption that online marketing is easy and cheap. Low prices worked in the early years of the expansion of social networks and internet search engines. Today, online marketing is extremely expensive. The goals of this presentation channel are changing, and it's impossible to build a business on it with only a small budget.

Let's look at some simple examples using basic numbers. Suppose we have an e-shop that sells shoes with an average price of $40. Our gross profit from one pair is $15. On Google Ads, we find that the keywords *"men's shoes"* or *"men's sports shoes"* cost around $0.35 per click.

These keywords are too general and will typically attract visitors who are just looking for information or to compare, rather than customers who are looking to buy something right away. This type of general keyword has a conversion rate of less than 1%. We need to get over 100 clicks to make a sale, so it will cost us $35 to make $15 – the investment is greater than the return. This basic calculation illustrates that advertising itself won't automatically generate a positive return on investment, ROI.

Many naïve business owners believe that one click will only cost them $0.05. After 40 clicks, it's likely there will be a sale and the business will make money on each pair sold. Great math. We invest $5 into advertising and make $20. Then we invest $10 and sell two pairs for $40. The business grows nicely.

Unfortunately, the reality is quite different, as the past few years have shown. Clicks are extremely expensive. If we only count direct purchases, we will rarely achieve a positive return. For advertising to make sense, we need to have a much more sophisticated system and broader objectives. Remember, only about 10% of companies succeed online. We need to be smarter than 90% of everyone else who tried a similar model. Setting up a website and obtaining products from a manufacturer is easy. Anyone can do it. The real problem is how to sell those products to make a profit.

PPC Advertising And Its Pitfalls

The marketing goals for online advertising have changed a lot. For large companies, it's primarily about protecting their advertising space and defending their position at the top. Giants like Amazon, eBay, Microsoft, and Walmart benefit from reputation, direct visits, and brand awareness. Online advertising isn't an essential source of short-term income for them. It's more of a strategic tool that is part of a complex and sophisticated business strategy. In addition, PPC advertising accounts for only a fraction of the turnover of these companies.

Examples. eBay Inc's profit is around $2.2 billion per quarter. In that same timeframe, they spend around $8 million on PPC advertising. PPC advertising accounts for only 0.36% of their profit.

Amazon has an annual profit of around $136 billion. Their annual AdWords budget is estimated to be around $144 million. PPC advertising accounts for only 0.1% of their profit. Amazon benefits primarily from direct visits, which account for almost half of its sales[27]. Clients are accustomed to looking for products directly on their website, reducing the cost of external marketing.

As you can see from the examples, large businesses spend only a small fraction of their revenue on AdWords advertising. A huge budget allows them to take up advertising space and keep the competition away. In proportion to their profit, it's not worth much. For a start-up entrepreneur who wants to take advantage of PPC, starting income will be very low and PPC advertising will eat away large margins of profit. It's worth considering whether using such a channel will pay off in the early phases of starting a business.

---

[27] www.sellerlabs.com/blog/10-amazon-statistics-will-shock-every-seller/

Let's look at practical examples and compare prices across different fields. PPC advertising initially seems to be a good first marketing step. Before jumping in, it's worth considering the numbers carefully.

Consider keyword bids for t-shirts:

cheap online t-shirts $2.60

cheap t-shirts $3.13

cheap print t-shirt $9.57

Given the price of t-shirts from $5 to $150, these cost-per-click prices are extremely high. Moreover, these are quite general keywords. For example, if we refine the keywords to:

buy discounted t-shirt

buy t-shirt on sale

Neither Google Keyword Planner nor SpyFu.com will tell us the approximate cost-per-click. This is because most large advertisers use more general phrases that cover these specific variations. We can assume the price is similar to the original ones. This places us in a situation where getting a few clicks costs more than the product we're selling. We have several options at this point:

- We need the average buyer to spend more than just the cost of a single t-shirt. Our system needs to offer the buyer something more – to upsell.

- If our average sale is $200, it's certainly better than selling a single t-shirt, but we're still making less than the amount of money we're spending on advertising. We need to figure out a way to attract a customer back to more purchases, but this time without expensive advertising. We can use cheaper methods, like remarketing or email campaigns. In this case, it's no longer a matter of the price of one purchase or the sale of one product. What we're interested in is the so-called *Lifetime Customer Value*. This is the amount of money a customer will spend with us over their lifetime of continued purchasing. If we sell shoes, our customers can come back every year, or even whenever the seasons change. If we sell service with a subscription or license, the client can use our product for many years. Examples of this are computer graphics tools, or accounting and software programs.

- Once we understand that a typical customer needs some time to think and compare their options – and doesn't usually make a purchase on their first visit to a website – then we know it's important to get this potential customer's email address. If we can manage this, we can reach the customer again, this time, without the high cost of advertising attached. If we want the potential buyer to provide their email or contact info, we need to offer them something valuable in return. What this is exactly will depend on the nature of the business. It can be a virtual product, (eBook, tutorial, free subscription, etc.) or a discount on a real product. For services, we can offer a free sample or a significant discount on the first purchase.

SpyFu offers even more interesting data. For example, it does a good job estimating the overall budget of companies that pay for keywords. For example, the phrase "cheap t-shirts" $1.6 million, $947k tisíc, $406k. Smaller advertisers spend between $5,000 – $30,000 on Google for this phrase. The smallest ones spend less than $5,000.

When we consider advertising in the field of T-shirts, let us consider the competition that is against us. It's very hard to compete with companies that have a marketing budget 100 times higher than us. If we still want to compete, let's choose another field where the big players aren't quite so powerful – fields where a personal approach and individual services are valued by the customer.

PPC ads for services

In some professions, the cost of PPC can get very expensive. Lawyers, therapists, and high-end personal trainers, for example.

Sample:

lawyer New York	$27.41
car accident lawyer	$167.61
personal injury lawyer	$100.39

A click-through for legal services can cost over $100. If we're not willing to invest at least $10,000, then the ad will be completely dysfunctional. Moreover, with a low invested sum, the data collected will be too small to have any statistical significance. It's much more efficient to invest a low budget in other marketing activities. Conferences, networking events, and seminars, for example.

General Keywords And Market Protection

PPC and ad-making authors agree that there isn't much point in investing in overly general keywords. Words like, *"kitchen"*, *"furniture"*, or *"marketing,"* for example. If you pay for such words, they will likely attract visitors who don't want to buy anything yet, rather they're looking for information. This type of advertising is expensive and inefficient.

Despite this, some companies are still paying for such ads. In the American market, I came across a paid ad for the word *"kitchen"* or *"kitchen furniture"*. You may be thinking to yourself that it doesn't even make sense to pay for such advertising, and yet, some companies do[28].

How does it work? When you create an ad for the word kitchen, then the ad has the potential to hit all who are looking for any phrases containing that word. For example: *"kitchen furniture New York"* or *"kitchen furniture designer"*. Ads built on this kind of general phrasing will hit all sorts of combinations associated with the original. Most of these clicks won't be from customers looking to buy something right away. The goal of a big advertiser is a little different. A huge budget ensures the possibility of efficient brand building. When a customer searches for anything related to the given word, they'll see a specific business ad. Repeated exposure increases familiarity and the likelihood that the customer will choose it when they do decide to make a purchase. The known usually wins out against the unknown.

---

[28] One possible reason may be, that the marketer has no idea what he or she is doing.

There is another reason why companies still pay for these expensive ads. It comes down to protecting their share of the market. When you're the biggest player on the furniture market and you have a million-dollar budget for marketing, then a big part of your job is to prevent anyone with a few dollars from competing with your business. How do you achieve this? Going back to the example of the word *"kitchen furniture"*. Whenever someone else's ad appears, even with a particularly specific phrase like *"brown wooden kitchen furniture in Long Island"*, your ad also appears. Large corporations don't optimize such advertisements very much. Their text sometimes has little relevance to the original search query. Often the ad will only show the name of the store, some contact info, and maybe a general discount offer. The goal of this ad isn't to sell anything at the moment, but to simply be seen and build ad awareness in the long-term. And, of course, to prevent hundreds of smaller advertisers from entering the field.

Through the examples in this chapter, I have shown that advertising goals and methods of implementation change over time. As prices rise, competition and margins fall, pressure on our creativity and originality increases. If you have a limited budget, it would be wise to consider other sales channels than online PPC advertising. However, this doesn't mean that PPC advertising doesn't work. It depends on how you define "work". If the goals include market protection, brand building, and reminders to clients, then PPC will work very well. If we expect to earn $150 from the $100 invested, this scenario is unlikely to happen. There are very few sectors where the immediate positive return, ROI, is easily achieved.

One of the areas where advertising can be used quite creatively and profitably is virtual products. For example, e-books, online seminars, subscription services, video courses, and so on. This type of product has a major advantage. There are almost no variable costs. Fixed costs in the form of product creation remain the same regardless of the quantity of pieces sold. Physical products are sold with a typical margin of 15-40%. Nearly 100% of the virtual product price is available. Therefore, there is no problem in investing 40-70% of the price in advertising. Check out the affiliate marketing website and see that virtual product authors commonly offer at least a 10% commission to their affiliate sellers. If you want a product like this to sell, online advertising is worth a try.

Website traffic is no guarantee of sales: A story

In the following chapter on marketing processes, I explain how important it is to successfully complete a sale. If salespeople are unable to close a deal, the whole marketing scaffolding will collapse, and the money will be lost.

Example. One of my first clients from New York was a small furniture dealer. Their budget for PPC advertising was approximately $6,000 a month. The shop owner rejoiced when he saw that the ads brought around 11,000 visits to the site a month. I wasn't in charge of setting up the ad itself, and I can't judge if it could be significantly improved. However, the owner, and later the store manager, had to deal with some unfortunate economic realities. There were plenty of website visits, but not a concurrent spike in sales. In discussions with the store manager, we realized that the cost of advertising was too much, and it was only bringing the company down. The owner, however, was adamant and insisted that the web traffic was necessary. The whole situation deteriorated to the point where even the owner acknowledged that advertising must be significantly reduced.

An interesting thing happened. Or rather, didn't happen. The number of visits fell from 15,000 to around 4,000, but sales hardly changed. Not paying for the ad saved the company about $70,000 annually with no loss of sales.

Another goal was to boost sales using social networks. This strategy didn't generate the income that the business management expected. The reason why this advertising didn't generate direct sales was the store itself and the vendors. Managers tended to micro-manage and employed underqualified people. Complaints proliferated on the internet: about the products, the management, even the delivery of the furniture.

I knew that improvement had to begin not on the internet, but in the store itself, and especially with the people in the store. However, the manager's willingness to change the perception of the shop and its management had to come first.

From Online Marketing Back
To Human Nature

For several years, online marketing has been increasingly effective and inexpensive. But the world is changing rapidly, and in the internet environment, more and more companies are trying their luck on social networks and online advertising. Although many don't get the results they desire, they stay and spend more money with the hope that things will improve. Technology has also moved marketing a great deal forward. It has brought thousands of new tools and strategies to sell more effectively.

People change much slower than technology. We're still social creatures, dependent on the community we live in. Relationships, humanity, emotions, and a sense of belonging are extremely important to us. Technology has taken us away from nature, and that's why we're fumbling in a new world that isn't close to us at all.

There are a huge number of automation tools on the internet that promise to save us time: Automatic responses on Twitter or Facebook, guest analysis, heat maps, user tracking, email and search analysis, and statistics. It can be difficult to navigate all the possibilities. However, all these options have one feature in common – they significantly limit real human interactions. On Twitter, I routinely get automatic messages from people I'm new to following. They don't even bother with a personalized greeting. Most corporate tweets are automated, and a live person checks the Twitter account once a week. Conversations are fading and companies use Twitter almost exclusively for one-way communication – as a promotional channel.

For Twitter, there is an automated strategy for attracting new followers. The principle is simple, a robot selects the accounts it wants to start following according to the company's specified criteria. If the newly followed accounts don't start following in return, the follow robot unfollows. On some profiles you can even see a description of this tactic: *"You follow me, I follow you"* or *"follow for follow"*. This type of strategy only makes sense for building a large group of followers. There is no relationship. Selling from an account like this isn't impossible, but it's particularly inefficient. It's purely a numbers game, with a decidedly small conversion rate. It might work for cheap products, on the order of just a few dollars, but it will be more difficult to sell larger items this way.

LinkedIn is also widely used by recruiters who actively add new potential candidates to their network. When you confirm the request and write a personal message, most of them don't respond, let alone greet you. LinkedIn groups almost no longer contain conversations, but only shared articles or products.

People believe that the world online will bring rapid business development, that everything will happen easily, and they can automatically run it all from their home computer. This assumption is incorrect. People are still people, regardless of the technology all around us. Valuable relationships are still conducted mostly in person, and importantly, still require time and work. Gaining the trust of another person doesn't come with a single tweet or impersonal request for a LinkedIn connection.

If you start to build your business using online tactics and fail, try to rethink how you would go about having that business in the real world. Meeting people over lunch, or at networking events and conferences may seem lengthy and quantitatively undereffective, but the quality of making personal contacts is much higher in the long run and has greater economic value.

Online tools can be great if they help rather than replace real people. Pre-scheduled tweets or Facebook posts are great, as long as you still have time to chat and respond to questions. Don't let a robot answer your messages. It's obvious to the recipient when there's no live person they're corresponding with. This potential client may even take offense. An automated message says to its recipient, *"I don't care who you are but buy my product here."*

There are already so many articles and e-books written about online marketing. I recommend not getting carried away with every new thing and always keep in mind that what people are primarily interested in is a person or company that has an interest in their problems. If you aren't interested in maintaining a social media site, then don't. Invest time and money in personal meetings and social events that have a much greater long-term impact on business.

If you're actively using online marketing, be as personal as possible. Respond to messages personally, politely, and let potential clients know you care. Customize your website and marketing to meet the requirements of your target market.

Simpson's Paradox - Watch Out For Data

Statistics can be used to generate misleading conclusions. Statistics is serious mathematical science and without a solid understanding, it can be used to create poorly constructed frameworks of reality. One pitfall in math (or any other field) is paradoxes.

When looking at data, there is always more than one way to interpret it. Try to interpret the data to get the opposite conclusion of what the data actually shows is absolutely possible. Before we can deal with this problem, we must be aware of its possibility. Let's examine some sample data.

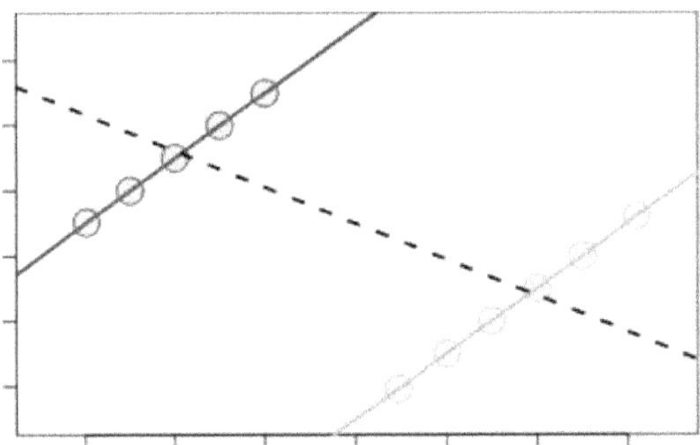

If we look at all points of the graph in the same way, then we can state that the trend of points is decreasing (dashed line). However, if we divide the points into two groups and examine each one separately, we find that the trend of both is growing. This graph isn't particularly illustrative for marketing, but it captures the essence of the paradox.

Let's look at a specific example from advertising, which we could easily encounter. Consider the results of PPC advertising.

	Men	Women
Views	50,000	50,000
Clicks	750	500
Clickthrough rate	1.0%	1.5%

Based on this table, we may come to the conclusion that advertising works better for women than for men, and we'll move the entire budget to a campaign targeted to women.

Let's divide the results into smaller groups and look at the data differently.

	Men		Women	
Age	18-24	25-40	18-24	25-40
Views	20,000	30,000	13,000	37,000
Clicks	720	30	460	40
Clickthrough rate	3.6%	0.1%	3.5%	0.1%

From the second table, we see quite different results. We divided the attendance according to gender and age, and we see that it's much better for younger people than for older people, and gender does not play the same role as before.

Dividing data into more and more groups may initially yield some results, but we run into a problem called the "curse of dimensionality" relatively quickly. There will be many categories and so little data that we can no longer draw any conclusions. Suppose we have two sexes - two groups. Then each sex can be divided according to age into 4 groups. We already have a total of 8 groups. Subsequently, we will say that we will divide visitors into 3 groups according to income. In total, we have already generated 24 groups. Some combinations may not contain any data at all. In short, it's possible that a visitor with a given combination of properties won't even appear.

The problem of how to properly divide the audience into groups so that they best describe reality is relatively difficult. It requires a combination of experience and experimentation. Different groups can yield different views of the same data. Then it depends on the ability of marketers to draw appropriate conclusions from the data, to optimize campaigns, and increase their effectiveness.

Digital Marketing Is Unbelievably Dynamic

In most areas of life, we take stability for granted. An athlete can spend years preparing for competition without worrying that the rules of the sport will change. The electoral systems of countries remain relatively constant. To some extent, it's possible to anticipate future political and economic situations because large changes are fairly rare. Business relationships also anticipate a certain degree of stability and reliability. We can predict the flow of money or the departure of employees. When our environment is stable, we can prepare for our long-term goals.

The field of digital marketing doesn't provide such stability and new developments can be dramatic. Unannounced and unpredictable changes can occur every day and fundamentally transform methods of business and marketing. For example, modifications to Google's search algorithms have been able to reliably destroy many internet projects. The new behavior of the algorithms has drastically changed the search results. Websites built on SEO and first positions could easily fall many pages down. A business built on organic traffic could lose two-thirds of its visits and orders overnight.

YouTube algorithms are also evolving rapidly, adapting to current trends and user preferences. Years ago, it was great to have a lot of subscribers because everyone saw new videos. Today, YouTube no longer shows new videos to everyone, but only to some subscribers, and monitors whether they're interested in a new video. If the video doesn't garner enough interest, additional promotion is reduced. As sites such as YouTube, Facebook, Twitter have to deal with an enormous amount of content, new approaches are emerging to select the best content for each user individually. The choice of content is influenced by artificial intelligence, which learns and develops over time. If we want to remain popular as YouTubers, we need to adapt our videos to algorithms - such as length, click-through rate, total time tracked, image quality, and so on.

The internet environment changes fast, and if we want to succeed as entrepreneurs and marketers, we have to keep up. Whether it's constantly monitoring developments and innovations, or experimenting and optimizing, or deploying new tools and tactics.

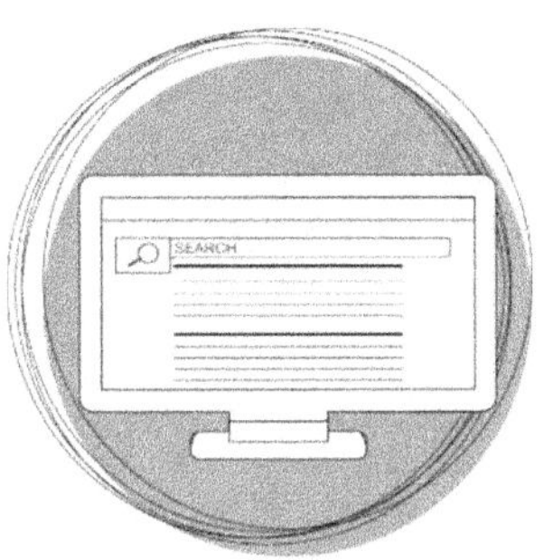

SEO – Search Engine Optimization

Search Engine Optimization (SEO) is a big topic for many companies. It's one of those subjects where the majority of people know a little bit, but only a minority of people understand it deeply and can formulate the requirements.

Clients often call with a simple request – to have the first place on Google for some given keywords. It's an overly simplistic and naïve view of how things work. I like to compare paying for SEO services to paying for a coach. Even the best coach cannot guarantee the victory of their trainee. SEO specialists, like coaches, can do the best they can at the moment with the talent and ability of the mentee (or the client's website in this case). But let's remember one important thing! We aren't alone on this racetrack. Other companies also want to achieve the top position in Google search results and also hire SEO specialists. There are only a few winners for each keyword, but there are hundreds of thousands of sites fighting for it. In addition, Google and its algorithms are constantly evolving. The rules and conditions for SEO are changing rapidly. Over the last ten years, there have been many fundamental changes in the field of SEO that have helped many companies but have also taken many out of business.

The position of a page within the search results depends on many internal (on-site) and external (off-site) factors. Internal factors are elements that we have the opportunity to adjust ourselves on the web. For example, content, internal page linking, sitemaps, metadata, responsiveness, site speed, and more. We can't simply influence external factors. For example, backlinks to our site and their quality, sharing our content (social proof), age of the domain and so on.

Search engines are becoming more and more capable of understanding text and content in general. Fifteen years ago, for example, a lot depended on the density of keywords on a page. When the website wanted to be at the forefront of the search for the phrase "sports shoes", it was precisely this phrase that had to appear frequently on the site. Of course, companies quickly understood how to create websites that manipulate the search. Google, on the other hand, does everything possible to ensure that search results aren't manipulated at all.

Nowadays, there is a lot of artificial intelligence in the background of search engines, which no longer examines trivial statistics such as keyword density. Algorithms are built to understand content in a similar way to humans. This means, for example, that algorithms recognize synonyms and related expressions. They know how to work with sentences and know the importance of words. For example, from the phrase *"Where is a Chinese restaurant in New York Manhattan"*, the algorithm understands that we're looking for a place, specifically a Chinese restaurant. Artificial intelligence handles that prepositions and conjunctions aren't as essential to meaning as verbs and nouns.

In 2019, Google introduced additional features to the search engine that bring the capabilities of algorithms closer to humans and greatly improve the understanding of common language. For specific sites, the result can be positive - we better meet the new search criteria and thus gain a higher position; or negative - our site falls in the results.

This chapter doesn't aim to explain SEO, as it's a topic that could easily take up the space of several books. We present it here for completeness and emphasize the basic principles that clients often don't know or have misconceptions about. As marketers and entrepreneurs, we should at least roughly understand SEO and be able to formulate real expectations. For example, if we want to hire an agency or specialist, we should be able to evaluate at least approximately the proposed strategy. Many tactics of SEO agencies are already obsolete and non-functional or downright unsafe. Education in such a dynamic field as SEO is undoubtedly never enough.

What Pitfalls Await Your New Web Site?

Nowadays, a website is crucial to almost every business. In some places, it's indispensable, such as for online stores, while in other cases, the website is more complementary, like for some B2B companies. A website should be approached according to the tasks it needs to fulfill. If we have an online store, then development is critical. Today, having a website is no longer cheap. There are beginner programmers and students who can create a trivial website for a few hundred dollars, but we can hardly expect high quality and professionalism. Larger web applications require many hours of development and troubleshooting which can be extremely unpredictable. In addition, the more complex the assignment, the more people will be needed to carry it out. As the number of people involved increases, so does the need for project management and the actual time spent working on the code goes down. A 1:1 ratio is also common, where half of the time is devoted to programming and the other half to documentation, testing, and project management.

Let's take a look at a shortlist of pitfalls that managers and marketers face on their new site, and describe some tips on how to overcome difficulties, or at least mitigate their impact.

Price differences between suppliers

When requesting a website, prepare a detailed and accurate entry. When you only have a vague idea of what is necessary from the site, the price can vary by hundreds of percent between potential suppliers. Companies with different levels of experience will look at problems and how to solve them differently. Experienced companies can draw from their experience of having solved similar problems in the past. In any case, the request you make will always be brief compared to the technical assignment the programmers need. For example, a client knows that he wants a project manager for his team. Developers will ask what objects he works with, how he is connected. For example, projects, tasks, users, timekeeping, rights, and so on. What happens when a user adds a project?. How does the project changes when a task is added? How is the task assigned to the user? Many similar questions need to be addressed before pricing. If developers don't ask you for these details and spend a lot of time analyzing them, their entire offering will be inaccurate – be prepared for the price to be up to twice the original estimate. Many projects will never be completed, or development will stop and start again and again.

Costs: immediate and future

A profoundly important and often overlooked factor in web procurement is considering current and future costs. At first glance, this comparison may seem meaningless. However, the cost of development is often governed by the following chart. A poorly written website can be cheaper in the early stages, but in the end, it becomes very expensive.

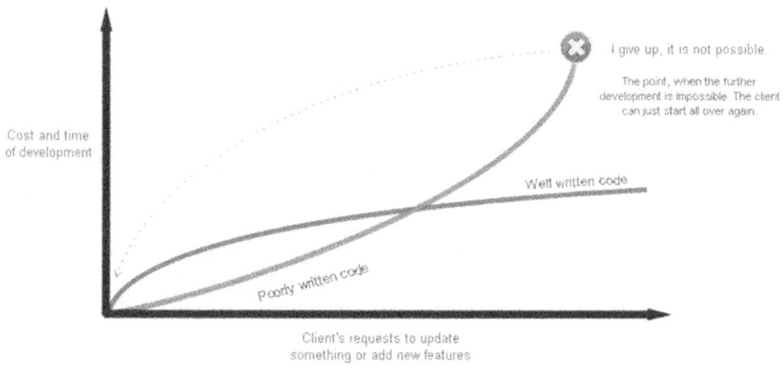

Well-written code, on the other hand, requires higher costs in the beginning. It takes a lot of time to come up with suitable concepts that will be applied throughout the development. The pitfall of programming is that you can start writing code immediately, but incorrectly. The client feels that the results are increasing rapidly. Problems will only become apparent over time. Each additional modification or extension is more complex and expensive. Development may occur to the stage indicated by a cross in the figure. The supplier will say that the required adjustment isn't possible or will cost an awful lot of money. The client has no choice but to find a new development team.

And because the code is poorly written, it must be started again from scratch.

During my practice, I've taken many phone calls from business owners whose programmer told them they could no longer complete the assignment. After looking at the codes, it was clear to me why this happened. It's no longer possible to expand the project with the same lousy system, and the best option is to start again and more thoughtfully.

Many companies, especially smaller ones trying to save money, will end up getting burned by this. As a result, they will end up spending more money than if they have been more concise from the start.

Developers should also be able to explain to the layman what system of work they use and why. If they don't have a good answer, they probably don't have a system and the result will be a disaster. In our company, I always spend an hour with the client explaining how we build the code, where it has advantages and disadvantages. Then it isn't such a problem to defend a higher starting price.

Agile development and technical specification

Creating a good technical assignment requires many hours of working with the client and understanding not only the techniques but also the business concept. This phase can't be underestimated. Something that may seem simple from the client's point of view can require considerable developmental effort. Many trivial features require complex background coding, deploying additional services, or gaining new knowledge. There is always some uncertainty associated with the development of new products. It isn't within our power as humans to estimate everything. The more capable a marketer or entrepreneur is, the better they can work with suppliers. It saves money and achieves results much faster. In addition, people who know the issue work better. I encourage my clients who manage their corporate websites to become familiar with technology and understand the basic concepts. This knowledge will have a positive effect in all directions.

Agile development means that the whole task is divided into sub-parts and they are submitted separately. The client approves each output and continues on. All costs and time are invoiced, and that part is considered handed over. Various design systems, such as SCRUM, are used for agile development. Depending on the type of project, the number of programmers, and the technology, the most suitable management system will be selected. There are several different project management styles with their advantages and disadvantages.

The task of the project management is to monitor the business assignment – Its conversion into a detailed technical assignment, the division of tasks between the teams, and, of course, meeting deadlines and handing over the individual parts. Even a small project requires some form of project management. Ad hoc approaches are typical for individuals, but they quickly lead to problems. Either the ability to complete the agreed parts is stuck, or the technical and business goals don't match. Sometimes, the client and programmer misunderstand the importance and priorities of individual sections which are not delivered in time.

Project support is most often provided by a software tool. There are several dozen quality and popular programs with various specializations on the market. Some are built specifically for software development, others for marketing projects, production orders, or services.

The topics of project management, building software, and websites are covered in several books. I don't have the space to describe them in more detail here, but I wanted to point out their importance. The assignment received by software companies is often generated by marketers. It's useful for marketers to understand things from the programmer's point of view. Wider knowledge is a prerequisite for better understanding between all parties.

Marketing Processes

Processes? Marketing Processes?

When people hear the term *"processes,"* many immediately get uncomfortable as they imagine heavy manuals with detailed instructions that will limit their creativity. Some go so far to say that processes are just nonsense.

In our approach to business processes, we emphasize a systematic approach to work, communication, and responsibility. For the company to fulfill orders in good quality, there must be a strong backbone in place. Room for personality creativity must be balanced with consistency and quality. The phrase *"marketing processes"* simply expresses that the goal of any work process should be client satisfaction. Any action within the company should be made with the client in mind. With this way of thinking, we can create a clear *why* for each employee. Furthermore, the employee understands why they're doing their job and has the freedom to suggest how to do it better. If there is no clear connection with the client, work becomes menial and pointless. People don't like unnecessary work, regardless of how well they're paid. If we give work without clear reasoning behind it, we unintentionally put our employees in the role of thinking robots.

When you do this to your team, there are two results. The first is a high turnover rate. People get tired of doing unnecessary work and quickly start looking for employment elsewhere. Currently, there is a record low unemployment rate in many countries around the world. People have plenty of opportunities to find a better place to work. Turnover is costly for the company, both in direct recruitment and training expenses and in indirect spending in the form of a drop in team performance and missed opportunities.

The second result of turning your employees into robots is inevitable micro-management. This usually ends up with all decisions concentrated in the hands of one or two people who want to control everything.

Why is micro-management so bad? Let's look at some consequences:

- ♦ It shows a high degree of distrust in employees, who are often persecuted for any missteps. This ensures:
    - o Employees become frustrated and want to leave.
    - o Employees who stay will work hard to avoid any conflict. They will look for the path of least resistance and will blame each other rather than take

responsibility for problems to avoid unfair consequences. Overall conflict and stress in the workplace
will increase.

    o   An atmosphere fostering creativity and independent
thinking will be lost. Innovation is necessary to stay
on the market long-term, and stress from micromanagement greatly reduces the potential of employees
coming up with new ideas.

- If you're the boss, micromanagement will put you in charge of every little thing; from sorting paperclips to answering emails. Perhaps this is possible in a small business with few clients, but your time will become increasingly limited. Soon it will be impossible to manage everything, and your mistrust of employees will block potential business growth. Expect high staff turnover and internal problems, both for the company and in your stress levels.

- You company = You. If you get sick and need to retreat for a month, your business will suffer. Forget about taking vacations; you won't be able to relax when you know every moment away from your company means economic loss. You will quickly experience burnout, a reluctance to work, and business stagnation.

- Micromanagement puts every decision on your plate, regardless of your ability to make the right decision. High-quality, talented employees are valuable because their creativity and differing perspectives push the company further. If you give up on this, it's only a matter of time before your business is overwhelmed by competition with new ideas. An individual simply can't know everything and can't make qualified decisions on all business matters without the help of experts.

Marketing processes ensure internal communication, responsibility, and decision-making with a clear concept and documentation. A marketing process without the consent of the employees and a good documentation procedure won't work in the long-term. The processes will often change as every new employee influences them. I describe it as an ad-hoc culture that somehow arises on its own and it's unstable. Let's look at how we can implement this with the example of a hair salon.

Business Concept – First Task

The term *"business concept"* is frequently used by business consultants and mentors, and I'm often asked what exactly it means and what it's for. I will illustrate with the example of a hair salon, which I worked on with a client.

The "*business concept*" is a group of values and goals that make up a successful business. The figure below shows what ideas fall under the business concept for a hair salon. We need to bring in a satisfied client base. Services must be rendered with a high rate of quality every time. The place itself needs to be looked after – someone needs to be in charge of the desired aesthetic. Finances of the company must be accounted for – rent, inventory, necessary equipment, and running expenses. Income and sales must be recorded and divided up among employees. The atmosphere and experience of our business should leave the client with a positive impression – what impression do we want to give?

We should have the whole concept figured out before we go any further. If we start building our company and then try to bring it together with an overarching concept, it simply won't work. Of course, we can always make changes along the way, but we risk losing time, money, and leaving a lackluster impression on our first clients.

Without a unifying concept, you're gambling on if and how the company will work. Maybe you think you will just start, and a concept will arise out of nowhere. Any spontaneous concept will be unstable, and it will change according to whoever is working that day and what their personal view of the business is. This will harm you as you will constantly be in a state of uncertainty and chaos, and it will harm your clients as they will never be sure what to expect from your business. Customers don't appreciate uncertainty; they prefer consistency and fulfilled expectations in exchange for their money. Companies that overlook this are left to compete by price alone – an inefficient and avoidable marketing strategy.

Concept design for a hair salon

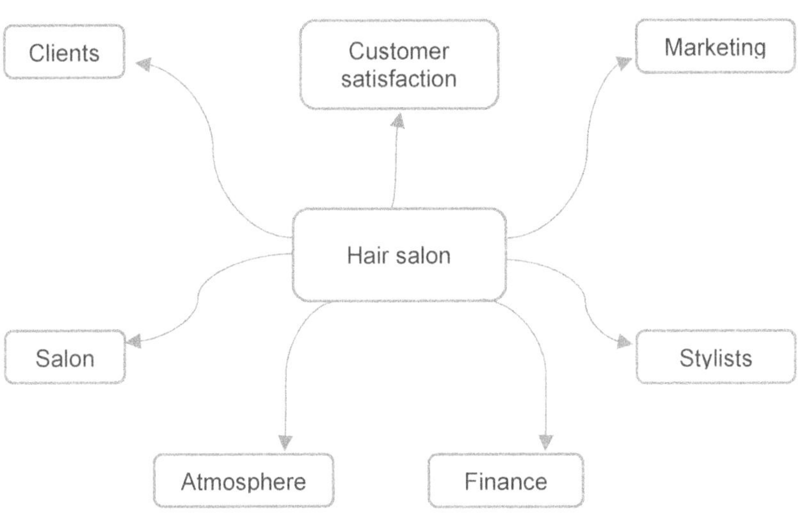

Clients

- Who makes up the target market?
    - Young women?
    - Middle-aged women? Businesswomen?
    - Men?
    - Families with children?

Considering the character and interior space of the salon, we chose to target young ladies and businesswomen.

- We want women to take from our salon:
    - The feeling of being pampered
    - The pride of devoting time to self-care
    - An overall greater level of self-confidence
- We build loyalty with clients
- We want our clients to return regularly
- We want our clients to recommend us to their friends

Customer experience

- Beautiful and clean environment
- A relaxing atmosphere
- Open and accommodating communication

- Details

  - Offering drinks

  - Fruit

  - Light refreshments

- Good location with easy parking

- Service of consistent quality

- A brand people will be interested in, connections to personalities

Customer experience and target market definitions are central to marketing. This directly shows how the space that the customer steps into must look, how to appropriately set the prices, and what additional services to include.

Marketing

- Online

  - Facebook

  - Instagram

  - YouTube

- Offline

  - Events

  - Promotions, presentations

    o   Gift cards and sales

    o   Brand awareness between clients and potential clients

    o   Partnerships

    o   Tours, shows, recognizable personalities

The presentation follows both the choice of the target group and our personal vision. If we want to service celebrities, then we must adapt our behavior and the face of our business to match our goal.

Salon

- Well-known and sought-after
- Status

    o   Associated with high quality

    o   Associated with known personalities

    o   Inspiration, quality, originality

How should clients perceive our salon? What do we want them to think? What terms will our business be associated with? Cheap? Expensive? Luxurious? Inspirational? Entertaining? The choice is up to us, but we need to be clear where we're going with it. If we aren't sure, we create confusion for our employees and clients.

Finance

- Rent

- Maintenance

- Facilities

- Profit

- Marketing

    o Organization of events

    o Sales

    o Salon presentation

Financing is an extremely important component of running a business and the management of it must not be left to a whim. Discuss the issue of finances with all employees, partners, and associates until everything is clear and agreed upon by everyone. I strongly recommend being sure all agreements are recorded in writing.

Salon space

- Facilities, equipment

- Planned services

- Guest service

- Cleaning and maintenance of the space

What will the interior of the salon look like? What element will create the atmosphere we're going for? How will it be furnished? How can we plan our color palette to match our target market? Are we interested in young urban women, or more of a conservative, older clientele? Will there be services for men as well? If yes, the waiting room should include reading material that will appeal to men – newspapers, sports magazines – not only women's fashion magazines.

Stylists

- ◆ Work relationships

- ◆ Tasks

  - ○ Cutting hair

  - ○ Marketing

  - ○ Responding to queries on social networks

  - ○ Participation in events

- ◆ Culture

  - ○ Communication

  - ○ Professionalism

  - ○ Attitude

  - ○ Responsibility

What kind of relationship do we want to foster between individual stylists? What type of contracts will they have? What kind of personalities best support our vision? We need to ensure all stylists can provide the same quality of service. How do we do this? All team members must know their tasks and responsibilities.

- Marketing
    - Presenting oneself online and in-person
    - Setting prices
    - Advertising
- Personal development
- Individual goals and vision

A marketing strategy will serve to elucidate and enact the previous points. We have a great plan and strategy, now we need as many people as possible to know about it. Marketing must follow the company's goals and our vision.

All these points form the outline of our concept. The main role of the stylist was described, as well as multiple smaller responsibilities and goals. The next step is to go into more detail for each point. The main goal is to indicate (in a measurable way) who is responsible for what tasks and what authority they get from their positions. This will serve to untangle future disputes, errors, or complaints that may emerge.

Example. One stylist gets sick but has a full schedule of clients for the week. We need to be clear about who's going to call the clients and explain the situation to them. Some clients may accept another stylist, but others may not. It isn't acceptable to surprise the clients with a different stylist than they were expecting at the time of their appointment,

The more detailed we get about how to resolve situations, the better. This is where the presence of experts can help a lot. If we're just starting out, we lack experience and may not be aware of what the potential scenarios could be. Outcomes don't have to be disastrous if we can react quickly and keep the client's benefit in mind. Any plan should be regularly revised and updated according to new experiences. The strength of your business lies in the power of you being able to handle situations and adapt to the needs of your clients and the market.

I will give an example of a shopping experience from my own life. Take care not to make simple mistakes. Many common errors can be easily avoided and provide the customer with a more pleasant experience.

The Story of How We (didn't) Buy A Mattress

As a customer, you can be mindful of various business practices and notice how other companies conduct themselves. Occasionally, you will notice flaws so enormous that you will wonder to yourself how the company stays in business. Let me give you an example I encountered recently.

My wife and I moved into a new apartment and needed a new bed and mattress. The first place we went to look for a mattress was a store called JK[29]. Our unusual marketing experience started here.

Shop #1 – we have nothing on sale

In the shop, my wife and I were just looking around at the mattresses when a salesperson came up to us. The very first sentence out of his mouth was: *"I'm sorry, but we don't have anything on sale."* There are two potential explanations for this. Either we looked so poor that the salesperson decided we didn't belong in the store, or the salesperson knew that all his products were overpriced and not reasonable to purchase except when there is a sale going on.

In either case, this was a terrible marketing approach as the salesperson wasn't at all interested in finding out what we were interested in or how much we had to spend. We had come to buy a mattress that day and, after deciding we were going to invest in quality sleep, we

---

[29] Name of the store intentionally shortened.

were ready to spend around $500. However, the salesperson gave no hint of effort to determine the cause of our visit to his store.

I took the initiative myself and told him that we were looking for a mattress in the middle-price range. The next unfortunate sentence he uttered was: "*I don't know what would be suitable for you, it depends on what you want.*" This is just as stupid as when you ask a waiter in a restaurant for a recommendation, and they respond with: "*Whatever you like to eat.*" Our case was more complicated than food. We wanted information so we could make a good decision.

We left the store without purchasing anything.

Marketing mistakes

- The approach of the store assistant was quite unfortunate. His first sentence basically tried to dissuade us from buying any-thing.

- We did not get any useful information regarding how to select a mattress, what the differences between the brands are, or what parameters we should focus on.

- The assistant mentioned discounts several times. It sounded like he felt guilty about excessive prices and had a moral obligation to inform us. As buyers, this approach can be appreciated, but not as the first thing we hear from the salesman. He was telling us that the price was too high before we were even interested in what the price was. This is a terrible approach to selling, and I am sure their boss wouldn't be too pleased.

It's interesting to see how many big-box stores invest in advertising on TV, radio, billboards, and the internet. Then, when you walk into the store, where the sales actually take place, the whole thing falls apart. I always advise my clients that business starts with people. When it comes to selling, employ real salespeople, not just people willing to stand around in the store. Having quality employees in the shop will reinforce strong relationships with buyers. This cannot be replaced by any technology or marketing tricks.

 **Tips** for marketing in business

♦ Employees need to understand that they are the most important part of marketing. If this piece of the puzzle is missing, all other efforts are useless. Training, mystery shopping, and sales bonuses can all be used to improve conversion rates.

♦ The basis of selling is to find out what the client needs and find them a solution. For an employee to sell, they must be able to communicate, be personable, and know the products they're selling. There is a big difference between an employee in a store and a salesperson. Being a good salesperson requires experience, knowledge, and a good attitude. It isn't a simple job by any means.

♦ Greeting a customer is nice, but it isn't enough. If we want the customer to spend money in our store, they must feel comfortable. If the customers don't have a positive feeling in the store, they will have a higher resistance to making a purchase, regardless of prices. The job of a salesperson is to create a pleasant atmosphere. For example, by smiling, showing a willingness to help, and knowledge of products. Increase the customer's confidence and deals are much easier to close.

♦ Coercion will hurt sales more than it will help. The more expensive the product is, the less effective coercion is as a sales technique. When buying expensive appliances, furniture, or a car, buyers value having as much information as possible before deciding to buy. They need to feel like they're making the right decision. The role of a good salesperson is to give them the information they're looking for to feel confident in their purchase. Examples:

  o How do clients make their decisions? Impulsively, or taking their time and weighing options? Different strategies apply to these different types of shoppers. For the impulsive types, phrases like, *"last-minute sale"*, *"last piece in stock,"* *"buy now and get a free gift"* work well. The thoughtful types need plenty of information, hard data, and the ability to make comparisons. This type is willing to pay more if the salesperson can convince them it's money well spent. Incentives like "sale ends tomorrow" have little to no effect. If anything, they may deter the buyer who now feels pressured into making a decision. After all, there will always be another sale.

  o How i mportant is price to the buyer? If it's very important, then we should compare products by price and emphasize the price-to-quality ratio. Or we can emphasize which models are the cheapest or best value. If the price isn't the deciding factor for the buyer, then we should present them with quality, service, extended warranties, and other extra options.

♦ It's always better to give the customer a few options to choose from. As we explained in previous chapters, people don't like to choose without having something to compare it to. Providing context for a relative comparison allows the customer to feel confident about their choice. Something like, *"this mattress for $450 is basically the same as this other one for $600. There is a big jump in quality between the $450 model compared to the $300 model."* Now the customer can select the most appropriate option for their price and preferences and leave with that *"I got the best value"* feeling.

Store #2 – Not interested in customers

After our discouraging encounter in the first store, we decided to see how our experience would compare with another well-known furniture seller. I had frequently heard the ad from this store on the radio.

We walked into the store and immediately noticed that the salespeople were uninterested in assisting us, and even had somewhat hostile expressions on their faces. About 8 people were working on the floor. Some sat at desks, others leaned against the furniture, and two women were just browsing on their cellphones. Terrible experience. Asking a salesperson with such demeanor questions makes the customer feel like they are an inconvenience. After approximately one minute, I knew I didn't want to buy anything from that place. I'm a tolerant person, but the disinterest from the staff was undeniably off-putting.

The radio spot fulfilled its purpose. They had achieved brand recognition and we even sought out their store to look for our new mattress. The whole marketing scheme fell apart with the staff, however.

I strongly recommend that store owners begin their marketing with training their salespeople. If customers already inside the store aren't comfortable enough to buy, any additional money spent on advertising will be a waste.

Store #3 – The sale starts next week

We decided to try a different location of the original chain store. They didn't have the mattress we wanted in stock but offered us something else that was in stock.

We found ourselves in the fourth location of this same chain store. This time, we knew straight away which mattress we wanted to buy, and the price was about 30% less than other models we had looked at. Even though I was fine with the price, and hadn't asked about any discounts or sales, the lady at the checkout advised me that I should come back in one week because the mattress would be on sale and significantly cheaper then.

It was almost the same situation as in the first store. I guess the salespeople feel that the products aren't worth the money at full price and so feel obligated to advise me against buying at the moment. If she hadn't said anything, we would have just bought the mattress at the price listed. As a customer, I appreciate a salesperson trying to save me money, but it still points to overall inappropriate price-setting. For the business, the salesperson's approach is terrible because she talked me out of purchasing while I was already in the store. Although I did in fact return and buy the mattress from that store, I could have just as easily gone elsewhere to make my purchase.

Take away from this purchasing experience

I hope the story of my experience illustrates how small marketing errors can lead to customer disengagement and loss of sales. Improving marketing here doesn't need any scientific calculations, just a little common sense, and a personal approach. The main lesson you should take away from this is that success depends largely on the last stage of the sale. All other marketing efforts rely on this final step. If you run a large company with millions in your marketing budget, it's worth shifting 10-20% of your budget to training and motivating quality salespeople. An enthusiastic client is more than willing to do marketing for free. Why not take advantage of it?

Positive Feedback, Yet Poor Results

As we have already mentioned, people tend to take feedback that supports their own opinion as the most accurate. Generally speaking, people don't like picking apart their ideas and decisions critically. This phenomenon also manifests itself in marketing as follows:

Let's imagine a company that isn't doing very well, for example, a restaurant, hairdresser, auto mechanic, or shop. The owner decides to get feedback from customers and asks them for their opinions. The owner finds that the responses are positive, and customers are pleased with the service. Sales still aren't doing very well; the restaurant is always empty, or people walk right past the store. A good business owner will try to find the source of the discrepancy.

Despite the positive feedback from customers, the store is failing. It's time to get some answers. Unfortunately, as often happens when one's ego is backed by positive feedback, the owner will insist they are doing everything right and the problem exists elsewhere, it's outside their control. *"Elsewhere"* can be anything – crisis, bad weather, fate, bad karma, phase of the moon, or some other nonsense.

Where was the mistake? The problem is that the owner asked the people who came! You'll always be able to find a group like this. Even the filthiest pub can find patrons who don't notice or mind the dirty environment, but when the group size is small, it will reliably lead to the business collapsing.

To get useful information, we need to ask the people we want as customers but who haven't yet come into our store/restaurant/salon. We have a choice: either take the praise of the small group that frequents our establishment but doesn't push us forward, or open our minds to critical feedback about what our business could be doing better to attract a larger clientele. Once we get feedback, we must take the appropriate actions to create change.

Entrepreneur, Technician, Manager

In the well-known book *The E-myth*, author Michael Gerber describes three roles that an entrepreneur must master. This model is easy to understand and illustrative, so we will briefly describe it here. For a successful business, the owner needs to effectively balance several roles and not let any fall into neglect. Every personality type naturally gravitates to some roles more than others. A business owner may throw themselves whole-heartedly into the administration that they have no time and energy left over for thinking about future development. This may not be a problem for a company built on strong business relationships – at least until a key customer cancels a contract and the company is completely unprepared. Lack of a new vision and reliance on a few clients is a common reason for bankruptcy.

The role of an entrepreneur is that of a visionary focused on the future and larger goals. They deal with ideas and abstract concepts. The entrepreneur provides innovation, creativity, and developmental direction for the company. They enjoy discussing various possibilities and diverse projects. They quickly find relationships to explore new opportunities and aren't afraid of the unknown.

The weak side of the visionary is seeing things through to the end. They sometimes lack finishing stamina and probably hate that stereotype. People with an entrepreneurial spirit have great ideas with lots of potential but hesitancy to commit to real action. They dream, invent, and develop many things in their mind, but these things tend to stay in their unfinished state. The business doesn't move forward.

The role of the technician is to solve problems in the present. These people take visions and ideas and bring them into the real world. If an entrepreneur has an idea for a product, a technician can assemble it, program it, or otherwise bring it into the light of day. Without technicians, there would be no final product for customers to buy.

There are two typical weaknesses of the technician. The first is a reluctance to work under management, and the second is a constant desire to improve the product. Technicians don't like having someone else tell them what to do. They may be reluctant to discuss what they're doing for fear of having their work sabotaged. For example, programmers often think that marketing departments are completely unnecessary and only complicate their lives. Technology isn't interested in vision, but in solutions. If the vision is vague, technicians can drive themselves into a frenzy making all kinds of small adjustments to the final product.

These constant efforts at improvement may at first seem like a feature. While this is undoubtedly a beneficial approach for science and research, it can be a direct threat to business. Too many improvements to a software tool can make it expensive and complex, and ultimately dissuade customers from buying and using it. Technicians don't much like to think about sales, and they aren't interested in the opinions of clients. They're focused on their own opinions about their creation.

The manager is the role that brings order. Managers pride themselves on their past success and proven practices. They don't like to accept change. The manager forms a bridge between the entrepreneur and the technician that determines the route a project will take. Without a manager, chaos reigns. The entrepreneur will dream, and the technician will constantly improve and overwork the product. The manager can help decide which features are and are not wanted by the consumer, keep an eye on the timeline for development and production, and ensure that the final product will be profitable.

The manager needs to be able to predict future trends using past data. They like to have prepared tables, estimate outcomes, and manage production. Managers don't like changes when they disrupt careful planning and present unfamiliar contexts.

At the same time, precision, planning, and insistence on established practices are also a weakness of the manager. Over management can slow development and prevent the company from reaching its vision. Managers are also nightmares for technicians because they require work to be completed according to a set deadline.

Each role – entrepreneur, technician, manager – brings different strengths and weaknesses to the company. For a business to be successful, it's necessary we balance these 3 components within ourselves, and in our workplace among employees who align with these different roles. What usually happens is one of these roles is underrepresented and companies suffer because of it.

When a strong entrepreneurial personality is missing, the company focuses on operational work. It may continue to do business with existing clients, but it doesn't develop. The owner may fear competition and try to compete by offering the lowest price, which makes earning a profit more difficult. Companies like this are too reactive and rely on only a few clients to keep them in business.

When a powerful technical personality is missing, the company often embarks on new ideas without a strong technical background. The entrepreneur has a vision and the manager draws up a business plan for it. The technical side of the project goes astray because there is no one skilled enough to pull it off. The project suffers from quality issues, misunderstandings with client expectations, and complaints about the product. Company representatives have trouble gaining trust as they clearly lack expertise. Informed customers and industry specialists will quickly reveal the company's incompetence.

Without the managerial personality, the company lacks order and will run into trouble to complete tasks on time. Deadlines go by unmet. The technician is never quite finished, and the entrepreneur is already coming up with a new project. Without a manager to oversee things, individual sections of the company don't know what they should do and when they should finish. Chaos translates into a lack of reliability.

Emails are lost, partners are left waiting for responses, deadlines inside the company aren't agreed upon.

For the marketing mindset, it's important you develop all three personalities within yourself. When a company is big enough, the roles can be divided among suitable employees. Communication should be prioritized between groups. The different aims of these personality types mean some minor clashes are inevitable. But in business, everyone must have the same goal – to deliver a great service or product to the client. The role of company owners will become not only the hiring of suitable people but also the design of internal processes for communication and decision-making that ultimately benefit the client.

Communication within the company

Communication is a key element of every company and the absolute basis of marketing processes. We will also look at a follow-up concept, understanding. In the chapter on personal marketing, we introduced the chain of communication, which we will return to again here:

- What I want to say

- How I say it

- How the other side interprets what I say

- How the other side reacts according to their understanding

- How I interpret their reaction

We can understand communication as the exchange of information, which doesn't guarantee understanding. Not understanding this concept causes various problems with a company. When individuals or teams in a company don't understand each other, it leads to conflicts that can affect the quality of service. It's the client who suffers in a situation like this.

Example. One medium-sized company I worked with had separate IT and marketing teams. Communication between the two was trivial at best. The IT responded to requests from marketing in the style of, *"send us what you want to have done, we will take a look at it in the next half a year or so."* Neither communication nor understanding was strong between the two. The IT department didn't know what the marketing team did, and so they undervalued them. Each system modification required based on client feedback took a painfully long amount of time to incorporate. The result of this was a low conversion rate for new clients and a product that didn't possess a solid position relative to its competition. The employees themselves admitted they didn't use their own service because it wasn't quite right. How can anyone successfully sell a product when the company's own employees think the product is flawed?

I emphasize to my clients that, in the first stages of development, the company doesn't need any experts in the field for expensive consultations. There is a huge amount of raw, but useful, information within the company itself. The problem is typically found in the lack of communication between employees. The company's own team is a fertile source for ideas and solutions. In many cases, the people who work in their field every day haven't had the opportunity to present their input, or their input has been ignored.

The cornerstones of understanding are a willingness to hear the opinions of others, to get to know each other, and to communicate openly. Getting to know each other doesn't mean cheap weekend teambuilding exercises with an abundance of alcohol. Many companies try to replace the non-existent communication between their employees by hosting such teambuilding events, which may only serve to annoy and demotivate employees.

Mutual understanding is best found in solving common problems together. All employees are in the same boat – they want to provide great services to clients, either directly or indirectly. Even the janitor and doorman are important for marketing. There is no "inferior" or "unnecessary" work if it has meaning for clients.

Allow people to get to know each other at interactive meetings where all parties are engaged. Topics for discussion could include future development, innovations, improvements to existing products or services, and ways to reduce returns or complaints to a minimum. Another option is to use personality surveys or logic puzzles.

Communication within the company requires systematic design and the involvement of more advanced tools known as "business intelligence". We, as business owners, are responsible for creating an appropriate information-sharing system. At the same time, we have to justify why we require individual steps. We should also be able to adapt these rules to if employees make justified requests for changes. Our employees shouldn't feel bullied or mistrusted in the workplace.

 **Examples** of the rules of communication

- For internal communication, use the XYZ system, which records all discussions and information flow. Everything has to be archived, even if employees change.

- Each team should have a designated team leader who receives requests from other teams and delegates them to team members. This team leader should confirm that a task has been received and provide an estimated completion date.

- Urgent requests should be addressed within one day.

- Client requests take precedence over internal requests.

- In meetings, everyone can express their thoughts, even criticisms, without fear of sanctions.

- Communications with clients are always polite and diplomatic.

There can even be more rules of communication, depending on the nature and size of the company. Rules should include responsibility for hitting deadlines and sending replies. There can even be fixed completion deadlines for various task types.

Understanding requires active listening. Employees should be able to express their views among themselves *and* to their leaders. Companies frequently have questionnaires that ask for people's opinions, but nothing seems to come from the feedback. Marketing processes should include the establishment of a system to use employee's opinions. Of course, the company doesn't have to implement everything employees come up with, but should at least listen, and respond with what is being implemented and what isn't currently possible, with concrete reasoning.

Companies suffer when employees become resigned to not sharing their ideas. They know that nothing will change. Leaders' reluctance to reliably listen drives away talented and motivated people. When employees struggle with bureaucracy every day, frustration and demotivation become rampant. Beware of the fundamental impact of such an approach: When a company doesn't value its employees, they won't value clients and the company will find itself in a bad position.

Example. Every year, large companies fill out job satisfaction questionnaires. Every year, one leader will come out with rave reviews and another leader with complaints against them. For years, employees don't see any change in leadership, even though one leader clearly isn't suited to their position.

A documented communication system between employees, between employees and their leaders, and between clients and the company is the basic element behind marketing processes. The concept of *marketing* is here on purpose, so that we always keep in mind the aim to deliver quality services to clients.

Marketing mindset and marketing processes allow you to build a great company both for yourself, your employees, and, of course, your clients. You will be prepared for economic and technological changes and your innovative approach will allow you to be a few steps ahead of the competition, with minimum effort on your part.

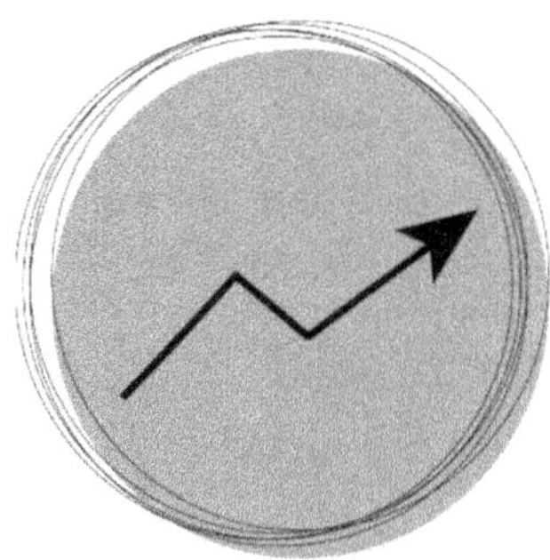

Never-ending Improvement

We have emphasized that having a marketing process is a great way to implement the marketing mindset in the company. A marketing process will bring attention to the systematization of task completion, continuous documentation, and the active involvement of employees in the development of the company.

To get started in implementing a marketing process that works for your company, I recommend looking into the well-known techniques of *"Lean Management"* and *"Kaizen"*. These techniques complement each other and bring a useful group of principles and tools for managing a company.

Kaizen is a Japanese word that means *"changes for the better"*. It's an approach to business that works with various tools. **Lean management** focuses on continuous improvement and openness to new approaches to production, technology, and leadership. Some of the tools we can take from these approaches are:

- **Six Sigma**. Six Sigma is particularly suitable for minimizing defective products by reducing variability in production. The basic principle of Six Sigma is using statistics and data to improve the efficiency and reproducibility of processes within a company.

- **5S**. Fives words that start with S, from Japan. They have been translated as *"Sort"*, *"Set In order"*, *"Shine"*, *"Standardize"* and *"Sustain"*. They emphasize the importance of order, cleanliness, standards, sustainability, and sorting out unnecessary elements. This is a general concept that needs to be adapted to the given situation. In a restaurant, for example, 5S would mean order, cleanliness, a dishwashing schedule, kitchen layout – choosing a place for the stove, fridge, and organization of cutlery, plates, and other equipment. Ideally, the setup will minimize unnecessary movement around the kitchen to achieve maximum efficiency.

- **Kanban, JIT**. Kanban is another Japanese word that translates to "billboard" and represents a concept for production. JIT is an abbreviation for "just in time". JIT is the goal that Kanban helps to meet. For production, this means that the company keeps the minimum necessary stock, doesn't produce when there are not commensurate sales, and uses the minimum amount of resources possible. It also emphasizes the need to check on the production process throughout, not only at the end. If an error occurs in the process, the damaged product should be removed immediately and not sent for further processing. The source of the error is detected, and the process is optimized to not make the same mistake again. Kanban is implemented in companies by software tools that visualize the production process. At each step, they indicate the level of certain parameters, such as the inventory, process speed, lag time, and a number of errors.

- **Hansei**. Hansei is more of a principle than an actual tool. In Japanese, it means *"self-reflection"*, which is perceived as the basis of all self-improvement. The essence of Hansei is that every employee can admit mistakes and work to correct them. This self-critical approach makes it possible to tackle mistakes more effectively and creates an atmosphere where everyone feels like equals.

- **Muda**. Japanese for *"uselessness"*, and a principle I used in writing about marketing mindset. The idea of Muda is to highlight how each function of a company must serve the client. For example, if we're thinking of adding some new features to electronics, we should start by asking if the clients are interested in these features. A similar principle applies to internal processes. We first have to ask ourselves if it will improve the customer experience. If not, we have to reconsider if our company needs it after all. Muda defines seven sources of waste: **transportation, inventory, motion, waiting, over-production, over-processing, and defects**. Another potential source of waste is not utilizing the human potential and employing skilled people for unskilled work.

I have selected just a few tools I hope will bring inspiration to your business. As you learn more about them, you will be exposed to even more new concepts, such a statistical process management, practical learning, agile product development, and visual management, among many others.

Implementing every new concept that comes along isn't necessary. Most of these methods are just frequently overlooked common sense. Take some inspiration and chose the principles that you identify with and which suit the needs of your business.

Choice, Feedback, Responsibility

Whatever system of personal management you chose, it's important you think about how the choice will strengthen the sense of personal responsibility among employees. Demands and exact workflow turn people into mindless robots. Managers often have the impression that they know the best way to complete tasks. While this may be true in the short term, by doing a given task, an employee soon becomes a specialist. Not listening to them is a loss for the company. There is nothing to be gained from forcing an employee to complete a task in a way that doesn't suit them. Innovation is more important than anything else. Business owners who don't understand this and adhere to the established *"we have been doing it this way for ten years"*, inevitably lose out.

Formulate tasks according to goals, rather than instructions for how to complete them. For new employees, get them trained and provide them with the tools to do their job, and leave the rest up to them – that's why they were hired after all. If they aren't capable of doing the job, find someone who is. To achieve the best results, provide your employees with the *why* and let them do the rest; don't impose endless restrictions and impossible rules.

Maybe you're wondering if I'm suggesting corporate anarchy? Not by any means! In a luxurious salon, it's expected that stylists adhere to high personal standards of grooming and appearance since that is what is expected from the clientele they serve. If they aren't on board with the concept, there is no way to work around it.

Employers want employees to be responsible, yet limit them with all sorts of orders, prohibitions, and micromanaging instructions. These concepts don't work together. **Responsibility is gained through choice**. What is the normal human reaction when they make a mistake because they were forced to use a procedure that doesn't work for them? "This isn't my fault; I was forced to do it this way." Even if the procedure was correct and the blame rightfully falls on the person who carried it out, people are still reluctant to take responsibility for actions they had no choice in. This situation is similar to when parents overmanage everything for their children – it ends in rebellion or resentment.

Where does this situation lead? When you can't expect personal responsibility from employees, there is only the carrot-and-stick method left. We find ourselves in a vicious circle. External motivation leads to reduced personal initiative and using the path of least resistance. This, in turn, leads to even more control measures and restrictions. Frustration and lack of motivation rise alongside the restrictions, while creativity, initiative, and responsibility evaporate.

Bad management style complicates the workflow of many companies without them even realizing it. At first, the company embraces high quality, motivated new-hires, and within two years disenchants them enough that they leave to seek employment elsewhere. Employee turnover is problematic, especially in terms of hidden costs and missed opportunities.

Be sure to implement a feedback system when you apply your marketing process. The flow of information must exist in all directions. From the customer to the company, between teams, between individuals on the same team, and, of course, between management and employees. Beware of half-hearted solutions! Many large companies use their own complex software solution, give out questionnaires to evaluate employee satisfaction, and organize workshops and team-building. For what? Almost nothing comes of these things. Questionnaires and spreadsheets are filled out, but the information goes nowhere. There is no system for using all the data that has been gathered, and that is a shame.

Marketing processes are so named on purpose to emphasize both marketing – i.e. focus on the client and their needs, as well as processes – and the answer to the question of what to do with the data. Data that isn't being used is worthless.

Creating a good corporate atmosphere and emboldening responsible employees, who will help us to continually develop, is up to us, the business owners. How well we accomplish this will reflect on how smoothly our company operates.

Meeting Standards Isn't Enough Anymore

For most products and services, clients have a wide range of choices, and they aren't inclined to make the same decision again after having experienced an unpleasant outcome. On the other hand, highly satisfied clients turn into fans that support the brand and take an active role in marketing for the company.

The question for entrepreneurs is how to get clients into the state of enthusiastic satisfaction. The answer is – always be personable with clients, take care of their needs, and pay attention to details. **Today, the standard for long-term success is not often met**. Let's look at some examples.

Example – a restaurant. Everyone has a favorite place where they like to eat and the price isn't the deciding factor. Think about what it is that attracts you to your favorite business. Is it the food selection, the quality, the beer, the staff, the ambiance? You have probably come to realize that many factors need to be next to perfect for you to consider the whole business as great.

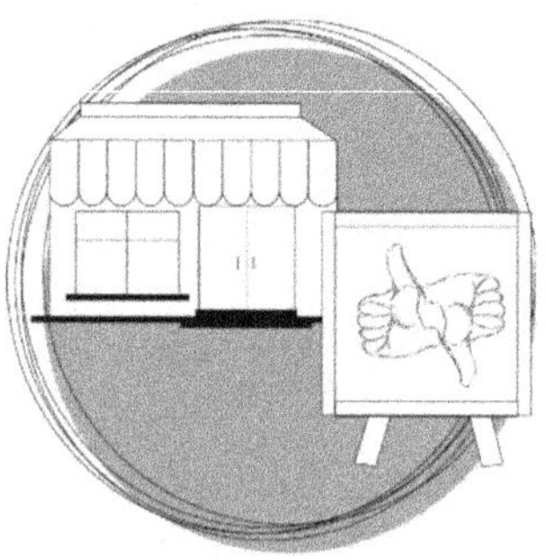

My wife and I recently visited a restaurant on the banks of the popular lake. The menu prices were high and suggested fine quality dining. When we asked the waiter if the fish were fresh, we found out that they were frozen. It would have been a huge disappointment to order such a fish. At once we had a bad feeling about the whole restaurant. A lakeside location where fresh fish is sold directly and the restaurant serves low-quality food at top-notch restaurant prices. Would you recommend such a place to your friends and family? Would you take the time to write a nice review on social media? Definitely not!

Example – hotel. The last time we visited a hotel, which boasted three stars, we had an embarrassing experience. On the one hand, it was a nice room with clean linens and a spotless bathroom. On the other hand, there were spiders all around the windows and outside. It was apparent that the employee in charge of cleanliness had orders to vacuum the carpet, change the duvets, clean the bathroom, but they wouldn't do anything outside their direct job description. This person fulfilled their tasks but didn't achieve the ultimate goal – a totally clean environment. For me personally, the spiders weren't such a problem, but I do know people who hate them and would have run out of the room screaming.

Example – internet provider. For some time, I was sentenced to receive my internet from the provider O_2. The experience with this company was terrible in all respects, but especially in terms of customer service. Every time I needed to get in touch with support, it turned into a 30-minute battle. First, you need to type in your contract number for an automated phone answering system, and once a live person picks up, they ask you to provide the same number again. If you fail to enter the data, you are disconnected and have to start the process over again.

After a while, I found another internet provider for our house. Coincidentally, this company uses the same cable distribution systems as O_2. The approach was completely different. They have an online chat on their website, where a pleasant operator is always available. Everything was solved quickly and conveniently. Report an outage, change the contract – everything without a problem. The difference in customer access was vast.

Example – Grocery delivery service. Today's technology can make it easier to work with clients and create a great impression. There is the customer service that demands you enter a specific identifying code, and when you're connected to assistance, the live person will ask you for the same code again. But there's another way. Once, a courier from a food delivery service unloaded bags that belonged to someone else instead of our own. I called support and I was pleasantly surprised. The operator who picked up the phone, according to my phone number, immediately knew who I was, what purchase I ordered, who the courier was, and where my order was currently located. I explained that there was a mistake. Everything took about a minute, and before long, the courier returned with the right bags.

I would like to emphasize two points from this story. The use of technology in this example was great; it made things easier for me and the operator, who didn't need to ask me any questions because all the relevant information appeared on their monitor. The support was fast and efficient. What is even more important is the human aspect of the support, the kind operator who had the opportunity to promptly resolve a mistake. All in all, what matters is not that a mistake happened, but that the mistake was easily and efficiently resolved.

Remember that just meeting the standard isn't enough. Bringing food to the table in a restaurant doesn't guarantee a satisfied client who will come back and recommend the business to friends and family. There are dozens of other factors: food freshness, quality of preparation, cleanliness, friendly staff, clean cutlery, warm plates, nice atmosphere, enough space around the tables that guests don't have to disturb each other when they get up, clean bathrooms, a pleasant front entrance without cigarette butts and trash, and so on.

All of this is part of the marketing processes. As business owners, we need to consider all the details and incorporate them into our concept. Then we can find the right employees with the same goals as us to set it all in motion. It isn't enough to do the bare minimum. Just bringing food to a table won't cut it.

In the next chapter, we will look at an interesting phenomenon that demonstrates the importance of attention to detail.

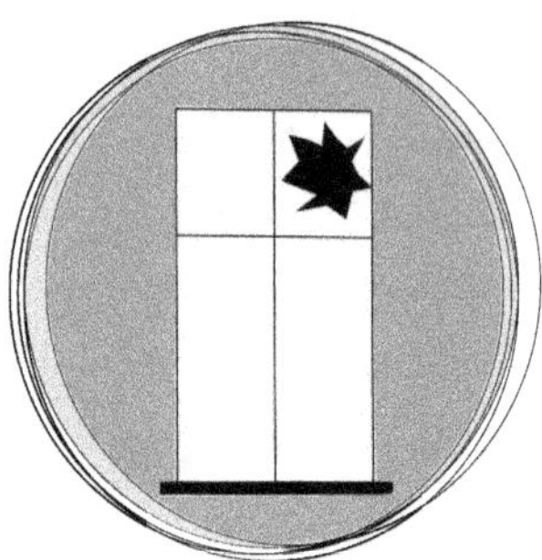

The Broken Windows Theory

In 1982, James Q. Wilson and George L. Kelling formulated an interesting theory that there is an increase in violent crime in neighborhoods where minor offenses go unresolved. If a broken window appears on one abandoned building and it doesn't get repaired, it's only a matter of time before another one is broken. This is followed by more broken windows, graffiti, property damage, and burglary.

The broken window theory[30] states that neglecting to take care of the outside of a building will gradually attract vandalism and an increase in crime in the surrounding area. When a building is left neglected, it's a sign that no one cares about the damage.

How does the broken window theory relate to marketing? The behavior of clients and employees are influenced by the same factors as the neglected building. If no one in the company minds the fact that

---

[30] en.wikipedia.org/wiki/Broken_windows_theory
www.britannica.com/topic/broken-windows-theory

the trash is overflowing, there are dishes in the kitchen sink, the carpet is covered in dirt, and the emails aren't being responded to promptly, then it's only a matter of time before one more "window" is broken. These small, overlooked details gradually build up in proportion without the people in the company even noticing. **But watch out! The clients certainly see it**! If we have dirty tables or poorly washes cutlery in our restaurant, our customers notice it and they probably won't return to our establishment.

A well-known Czech TV chef[31] said the following, which nicely sums all this up:

"If there is a mess in the kitchen, whatever the reason, it automatically means that your food is terrible. Automatically!"

Cleanliness, taking care of the premises, repairing things that are broken, polite behavior, and clear communication all contribute to maintaining a high quality of service. At first glance, this may seem unrelated to order, but our perception of our atmosphere influences our decision-making. When one employee flagrantly disregards our company standards, it will probably only be a matter of time until others join them. The subsequent reluctance to comply with standards may directly affect the customer experience.

How can we do better? Look at your business and try to find all the *"broken windows"*. Fix these little things immediately because

---

[31] A very similar TV show to Gordon Ramsey's *Kitchen Hell*.

they can snowball and get out of control. In previous chapters, we described continuous improvement techniques. These are very useful for a business owner to know and implement in their workplace.

Let's remember that the standard is no longer enough. Customers want more. It may sound like an awful lot of work and a lot of risks – but there's good news! Most entrepreneurs don't want to deal with small things at all and consider them "unnecessary details". Therefore, only a minority of them are successful. If you chose to pay attention to these small details and never stop being critical of your standards, you will earn yourself a competitive advantage that other companies will be hard-pressed to identify or replicate.

Crisis Communication

Crisis communication, as the name suggests, is about informing customers and suppliers when a crisis occurs. A crisis can be anything negative that disrupts business – data leakage, attack ads, problems with production, mistakes, controversial ad campaigns, and so on.

Many companies, even big ones, don't bother with the preparation of crisis communication. When a crisis occurs, it will be such a shock that they fail to react or even make the situation worse. The first rule in crisis communication is to prepare for it in advance. Divide up responsibilities and forms of communication with media, internet portals, and social media. All participants should be clear about what to say and how to say it. It's helpful to practice by simulating a problem to test how the team responds.

Some companies are able to use crises to strengthen their client's trust. Yes, a mistake may have been made initially, but by taking the initiative to fix it the company shows its clients that it's reliable. No one is perfect and mistakes happen. The willingness and effort to resolve a situation for the benefit of the client is the most important aspect here.

A few tips for crisis communication

♦   Analyze the situation

♦   Admit to the mistake, be honest, don't look for a scapegoat

♦   Apologize

♦   Make things right as quickly as possible

♦   Keep clients informed through the entire course of the crisis and be transparent – don't hide bad news

♦   Cooperate with clients, suppliers, and even external investigators

What *not* to do during a crisis

♦   Lie or obscure the reality of the situation

♦   Trivialize the problem or its potential consequences

♦   Blame clients or suppliers

♦   Be arrogant

- Be silent

- Provide minimal information, fail to communicate with media sources, or provide conflicting information to different sources

You should prepare for crisis communication, even if you only run a small business. Delayed invoices, complaints, product errors, late delivery, website errors, unrecognized discounts, controversial ad campaigns, and direct brand attacks are a few things that could cause a crisis. At least come up with a framework of action for a crisis and delegate power and responsibilities to individual employees. This is especially important for employees tasked with communicating with the media. The response should be swift and consistent across all channels.

Pareto Principle And Price's Law

The Pareto principle, also known as the 80/20 rule, is a relatively well-known observation of human productivity. Simply put, 20% of our activity generates 80% of our results. Alternatively, 20% of people make up 80% of the value in a company. This is probably how most people have heard of Pareto's principle, but many people are unaware of the further implications it had for business or careers.

The Pareto principle isn't a proven law of nature, but an observation that is reliably repeated. Humans tend to assume linear fluctuations between different inputs and outputs and a statistical normal distribution. Unfortunately, the world is much more complicated and linear dependence doesn't always apply. Nonlinear dependencies can be so unintuitive that many people have great difficulty understanding the context and automatically draw wrong conclusions.

A very important element in understanding productivity is that a minority of activities will yield most of the results. At the same time, however, we can't get rid of the majority, because then the same principle would apply to a reduced group. Imagine that you're drawing a picture of a car and the entire project takes 10 hours. It will most likely be clear after two hours what will be on the picture. The rest of the time you complete the details. However, there's no way that you could eliminate the "less productive" eight hours because then the picture wouldn't be as good.

A business must think about the need to identify a few important factors that generate the greatest returns. Again, the remaining activities cannot be completely discarded as their results would be missing somewhere.

In internet campaigns, whether advertising, blogs, or social networks, we also encounter disparity between the number of total campaigns and the number of successful ones. Look for key factors that unite the success of the few and apply them to your operations. The Pareto Principle is still in effect, but by isolating the most powerful sources of success, marketing can be made more effective and more profitable.

Price's Law (authored by Derek J. de Solla Price) describes productivity efficiency as follows: The square root of the number of people in a team generates 50% of the results. When we have 9 people in a team, 3 of them will create 50 of all results. When we increase the number of team members to 100, only 10 of them will produce half the results.

Price's Law is particularly interesting, especially for leading larger teams, where we can easily identify key people who not only generate the majority of returns but also motivate and develop other members of the group. Large companies often hire managers without the necessary soft skills. They don't pay enough attention to the people in the team and they lose key personalities and thus the productivity of the whole company suffers. Large companies and corporations often buy successful start-ups because a start-up with a small team can be much more productive with the same budget. There are plenty of examples of mergers between successful corporations and smaller start-ups – Facebook bought Instagram, Google took over YouTube, Microsoft bought LinkedIn and GitHub.

When leading a team of five or more people, carefully identify key people, and take care of their satisfaction. Not only financial security, but also recognition, responsibility, and opportunity for growth. People have different requirements and their fulfillment depends on their motivation and willingness to stay in the company. The higher the employment in the economy, the greater the competitive struggle of companies for key people. Unfortunately, many companies apply a management system that directly expels productive workers.

Let's remember that the differences in productivity between individuals can be vast and it's impossible to create a perfectly fair system. Whether in terms of salary, position, assigned tasks, responsibility, or people management, everything is perceived subjectively and under the influence of emotions. Company culture should take these aspects into account, or risk significant internal conflicts and overall loss of team productivity.

A Few Tips for Your Next Steps

Through the course of this book, we have learned about the basics of marketing mindset, and how to connect this knowledge to motivation, personal marketing, and presenting work online. We emphasize the importance of providing the client with value and a human approach. The goal of this book is to point out the diversity of contexts that makes marketing a much more complex process than many textbooks suggest.

Now it's your turn. A book is useless unless it can inspire the reader to act. Even if at this moment, you don't have all the knowledge to overcome any potential obstacle you may face in the future, you can't let fear stand in the way of success. The first step is to understand your inner motivation, and then get to work. If you're thinking about starting your own business, get started right away. Our company can give you a helping hand and help you to develop a concept that will guide you toward smarter decisions and faster development.

Perhaps you're looking for better orientation within your motivation or need to rekindle the lost spark of your passion. In any case, we can recommend a suitable coach or personal development expert.

If you already own a small business and want to develop it to become less dependent on you, we can help you to develop a detailed business concept and document your internal processes. You get a high-level view of your business and can make more effective decisions.

Connecting people and marketing is the foundation of our work. If this approach appeals to you and you want to implement new marketing processes in your company, be sure to contact us. Your leadership will be much more efficient, business more productive, and your employees more satisfied at work. And of course, all this will be appreciated by your satisfied clients.

Finally, we would like to ask you for your feedback, either by e-mail or via social media. We look forward to your opinions and suggestions.

The author Peter Matisko and the team of Cyberma wish you the best of luck in your career and personal life.

About the author

Peter Matisko graduated from the Czech Technical University in Prague, with a specialization in control engineering, cybernetics, and applied mathematics. In 2009 he completed his engineering studies and in 2013 he defended his doctoral thesis in the field of control engineering and robotics. As a born tech enthusiast, he wanted to work in the business of technology throughout his studies. The study of business and marketing led him to projects in the field of e-commerce, where he continued to develop skills in business and marketing. His first contracts in marketing came soon after, and since 2012 he has been working as a consultant to help businesses with the marketing mindset, technology, and overall business development.

Since 2018, Peter has been teaching at the University of Economics and Management Prague, where he lectures on marketing and technology. Peter has worked on dozens of projects with small and start-up entrepreneurs looking to build successful businesses. His unique combination of technical expertise and analytical thinking, coupled with personality and marketing development, has helped him to create company concepts, marketing campaigns, internal processing, and provide personal mentoring.

Get connected: www.linkedin.com/in/petermatisko

References

Ariely D. (2008). *Predictably irrational*, HarperCollins.

Burnett J. (2012). *How to Avoid Random Acts of Marketing: A Plan for Small to Midsized Legal Firms*, Kindle Edition.

Collins J. (1994). *Built to last*, HarperCollins.

Collins J. (2001). *Good to great*, HarperCollins.

Cowey S. R. (1990). *Principle-Centered Leadership*, Rockefeller Center.

Cowey S. R. (2004). *The 7 Habits of Highly Effective People: Powerful Lessons in Personal Change*, RosettaBooks.

Finklestein R. (2010). *49 marketingových tajemství pro zaručené zvýšení prodeje*, Press.

Gaudet C. E. (2014). *The Predictable Profits Playbook: The Entrepreneur's Guide to Dominating Any Market – And Staying On Top*, Kindle Edition.

Gerber M. E. (2004). *The E-Myth*, HarperCollins.

Haden N. K. (2015). *The 9 Virtues of Exceptional Leaders: Unlocking Your Leadership Potential*, Kindle Edition.

Hopkins R. (2012). *Team Covenant*, Xlibris Corporation.

Janouch V. (2014). *Internetový marketing*, Albatros Media.

John R. S. (2010). *The 8 Traits Successful People Have in Common: 8 to Be Great*, Trait of Thought Arts.

Jones G. and R. Gorell (2012). *50 Top Tools for Coaching: A Complete Toolkit for Developing and Empowering People*, Kogan Page.

Kopřiva P., J. Nováčková, D. Nevolová and T. Kopřivová (2012). *Respektovat a být respektován*, Spirála.

Lewis J, Rees-Jones A., Simonsohn U. and J. P. Simmons. *Diminishing Sensitivity to Outcomes: What Prospect Theory Gets Wrong about Diminishing Sensitivity to Price*.

Litner J. (2020). *How to handle impostor syndrome*. Medical News Today

Ludvík P. (2013). *End Procrastination*, Jan Melvin.

Maltz M. (1960). *Psycho – Cybernetics*, Prentice Hall.

Princ M. (2013). *Jak uspět při obchodním telefonování*, Grada.

Rogers M. Everett (1962). *Diffusion of Innovations*.

Scott D. M. (2008). *The New Rules of Viral Marketing*.

Sinek S. (2009). *Start with Why: How Great Leaders Inspire Everyone to Take Action*, Penguin Books.

Sutton R. I. (2010). *Good Boss, Bad Boss*, Business Plus.

Templar R. (2005). *107 zlatých pravidel úspěšného manažera*, Grada.

Urban J. (2010). *10 nejdražších manažerských chyb*, Grada.

Vaňhara J. (2009). *Podnikání v USA*, SnowMouse Publishing.

Wharam J. (2008). *Emotional intelligence*, John Hunt Publishing.

Whitmore J. (2009). *Coaching*, Management Press.

Wickman G. (2007). *Traction*, BenBella Books.

Wolfová D. and R. Merkle (1997). *Jak rozumět svým pocitům a jak překonávat problémy*, Pragma.

Internet sources

support.google.com/adwords – materiály k certifikaci PPC

thenextweb.com/entrepreneur/2015/02/07/8-10-statistics-totally-made/#.tnw_dYLerYZM

www.sba.gov/sites/default/files/FAQ_Sept_2012.pdf

feedit.cz/2017/04/26/25-firem-v-cr-zanika-nejcasteji-v-patek-jaky-den-je-nejvhodnejsi-pro-jejich-zalozeni/

www.kickstarter.com/help/stats

www.shoptet.cz/stav-e-commerce-v-cr-2015/

www.cbinsights.com/research-reports/The-20-Reasons-Startups-Fail.pdf

Mark J. G., S. Voida and A. V. Cardello (2012). „A Pace Not Dictated by Electrons": An Empirical Study of Work Without Email. www.ics.uci.edu/~gmark/Home_page/Research_files/CHI%202012.pdf

en.wikipedia.org/wiki/Barnum_effect

en.wikipedia.org/wiki/Bertram_Forer

www.psychologytoday.com/blog/sideways-view/201411/weve-got-something-everyone-the-barnum-effect

Shamsi T. I. and E. Horvitz (2007). Disruption and Recovery of Computing Tasks: Field Study, Analysis, and Directions. http://erichorvitz.com/CHI_2007_Iqbal_Horvitz.pdf

BBC (2005). 'Infomania' worse than marijuana

news.bbc.co.uk/2/hi/uk_news/4471607.stm

Salary.com. Why & How Your Employees are Wasting Time at Work business.salary.com/why-how-your-employees-are-wasting-time-at-work/

Salary.com. Facebook & Too Many Meetings Top the List of Employee Time-Wasters. http://business.salary.com/why-how-your-employees-are-wasting-time-at-work/

www.capitalandconflict.com/market-updates/money-morning-share-tips-nokia-10601/

www.brightlocal.com/learn/local-consumer-review-survey/

blog.hubspot.com/marketing/chartbeat-website-engagement-data-nj

Roberta Vaele: scholar.google.com.au/citations?user=lbLJGzYAAAAJ

investors.ebayinc.com/releasedetail.cfm?ReleaseID=1021956

www.spyfu.com

sellerlabs.com/blog/10-amazon-statistics-will-shock-every-seller/

en.wikipedia.org/wiki/Impostor_syndrome

fortune.com/2015/04/02/quit-reasons/

www.kaizenworld.com

www.lean.org/WhatsLean/

www.leanproduction.com/top-25-lean-tools.html

www.etymonline.com/index.php?term=inspiration

enhancedmotivation.com/movere

en.wikipedia.org/wiki/Broken_windows_theory

www.britannica.com/topic/broken-windows-theory

www.wired.com/2012/04/5-reasons-why-nokia-lost-its-handset-sales-lead-and-got-downgraded-to-junk/

www.newyorker.com/business/currency/where-nokia-went-wrong

Conover A. Adam ruins everything: www.youtube.com/user/collegehumor

347